A Game Plan for Life

BY JOHN WOODEN

They Call Me Coach (with Jack Tobin)

Practical Modern Basketball

Wooden: A Lifetime of Observations and Reflections on and off the Court (with Steve Jamison)

Coach Wooden One-on-One: Inspiring Conversations on Purpose, Passion, and the Pursuit of Success (with Jay Carty)

My Personal Best: Life Lessons from an All-American Journey (with Steve Jamison)

Coach Wooden's Pyramid of Success Playbook: Applying the Pyramid of Success to Your Life (with Jay Carty)

Coach Wooden's Pyramid of Success: Building Blocks for a Better Life (with Jay Carty)

Wooden on Leadership (with Steve Jamison)

The Essential Wooden: A Lifetime of Lessons on Leaders and Leadership (with Steve Jamison)

BY DON YAEGER

Never Die Easy: The Autobiography of Walter Payton (with Walter Payton)

Running for My Life: My Journey in the Game of Football and Beyond (with Warrick Dunn)

It's Not About the Truth: The Untold Story of the Duke Lacrosse Case and the Lives It Shattered (with Mike Pressler)

Turning of the Tide: How One Game Changed the South (with Sam Cunningham and John Papadakis)

Ya Gotta Believe!: My Roller-Coaster Life as a Screwball Pitcher and Part-Time Father, and My Hope-Filled Fight Against Brain Cancer (with Tug McGraw)

A Game Plan for Life

· ·

THE POWER OF MENTORING

John Wooden

and

Don Yaeger

NEW YORK · BERLIN · LONDON

Published by Bloomsbury USA, New York

All papers used by Bloomsbury USA are natural, recyclable products made from wood grown in well-managed forests. The manufacturing processes conform to the environmental regulations of the country of origin.

LIBRARY OF CONGRESS CATALOGING-IN-PUBLICATION DATA

Wooden, John R.
　A game plan for life : John Wooden's lessons on mentoring / coach John Wooden and Don Yaeger.
　　　p. cm.
　Includes bibliographical references and index.
　ISBN 1-59691-701-6 (hardback : alk. paper)　1. Wooden, John R.
2. Basketball coaches—United States—Biography.　3. Mentoring.
4. Conduct of life.　I. Yaeger, Don.　II. Title.
　GV884.W66W66 2009
　796.323'2—dc22

2009022822

First U.S. Edition 2009

1 3 5 7 9 10 8 6 4 2

Interior design by Rachel Reiss
Typeset by Westchester Book Group
Printed in the United States of America by Quebecor World Fairfield

To Nellie, who spent her lifetime teaching me great lessons. Thanks for being my love...and my mentor! —John Wooden

To my daughter Madeleine. I hope you will find mentors in your life that will have as positive an impact on you as Coach Wooden has had on me. Always remember to surround yourself with friends who are headed in a positive direction. And one last thought from Coach to you: Make each day your masterpiece! —Don Yaeger

Contents

· · · · · · · · · · · ·

Foreword

John C. Maxwell

I HAVE ADMIRED John Wooden for as long as I can remember. Growing up, basketball was my passion. From the time I was ten years old until I graduated from high school, playing ball was the only thing I ever really wanted to do. I could find any excuse to shoot some baskets or to play in a pickup game. I captained my high school team as a senior, and I went on to play ball for a small college.

While I was playing on that very small stage in central Ohio, Coach Wooden was leading some of the greatest college teams of all time on the national stage. He set the gold standard as a coach and leader. My respect and admiration for him are hard to express. He has not only achieved the heights in his profession, having won ten national championships and being named ESPN's Greatest Coach of the Twentieth Century, but he has also lived with integrity and honor. Never in the world would I have guessed back then that I would someday get to meet Coach Wooden. It's even more astounding that he would agree to mentor me.

Mentoring has always been critical to me. My first mentors were my parents. My father, Melvin, mentored me in character and work ethic when I was a boy, just as John Wooden's father mentored him.

When I got started in my career, I went looking for other mentors to teach and guide me. I wanted to learn things I couldn't find in any books back then. For several years my wife and I planned our summer vacations based on which leaders agreed to give me thirty minutes of their time in exchange for what was then a large sum of money for me. As time went by, I was able to find other significant mentors.

When I was in my early thirties, I started mentoring members of my staff. And at about that time others began asking me to teach and mentor them, too. That's how I got started as a conference speaker and writer. And I continue to personally mentor a handful of individuals on a regular basis.

I'm more than sixty now, and I still seek out people from whom I want to learn. And my favorite person to meet with is John Wooden.

For the past several years, I've had the privilege of spending a day with Coach Wooden every six months or so. We usually eat lunch at his favorite restaurant, and then we retreat to his apartment. He is such a gracious man, humble, and still as sharp as can be. And he is always committed to teaching. I have learned a lot from him in a short time.

Whenever one of my meetings with Coach Wooden approaches, I spend a lot of time thinking about the questions I will ask him. I practice my 10x principle. I spend ten minutes preparing for every minute I expect to spend with him. I want to glean every bit I can from him during our time.

Recently when I was with him, Coach looked at my yellow legal pad full of questions and realized that as much as I was enjoying just chatting with him, he sensed that I wanted to get to the questions I'd prepared.

"John, let's just get on it," he said with a smile as he pointed to my pad. And then he told me, "Of all the people who come to me, no one prepares like you prepare, and I want to talk about everything you have there."

That's an incredible compliment coming from the man who planned down to the minute every basketball practice he ever led. I found it very humbling.

I was humbled again when Coach Wooden invited me to write the foreword to *A Game Plan for Life*. I've read and reread every book he has written. They "mentored" me long before I got to meet Coach Wooden face-to-face. So of course I told him I would be honored to do so, not only out of love and respect for him, but also because the subject is so important.

As you read this book, you will greatly benefit from Coach's wisdom. In the pages that follow are practical tips on how to approach the art of mentoring as both a mentor and recipient of mentoring. The first half of the book tells the stories of seven mentors who impacted Coach; the second half shares stories about seven people whose lives he has helped to shape.

There's so much to learn from this man who has had such a great impact on so many lives. He knows how to teach, and even at more than ninety years of age, he continues to learn. Those qualities have made John Wooden an American treasure and a great mentor to me. And now thanks to this book, he can be a mentor to you.

PART I

The Seven Mentors in My Life

CHAPTER 1

· · · · · · · · · · · ·

What Is a Mentor?

OVER THE YEARS, I HAVE WRITTEN books about basketball, about leadership, about coaching, and about my life. But this may well be my most important work. While I made my living as a coach, I have lived my life to be a mentor—and to be mentored!—constantly.

When I reflect on my life, I find that the people who stand out are the ones who challenged me with words and inspired me with actions. They taught and they showed and they modeled and they lived and they shared. This book, then, is my tribute to those men and women whose lives, philosophies, and faith all shaped my own.

Many people look at mentoring as some kind of assignment, something you sign up to do at a local school. And while that type of mentoring is important, that is only one form of it. Mentoring can be any action that inspires another; every time we watch someone and make a mental note about that individual's character or conduct, we're being mentored. Every time you greet the grocery store checker with a smile or pick up a piece of litter or pat someone on the back, someone may very well be watching you. It's really about the choices we make—decisions about how we will observe the world and decisions we make about the way we will act in it. Mentoring can happen at any time or place. It is both something we receive and something we give.

Mentors are all around us; they are everywhere we look. Anywhere there is a sharing of knowledge or a teaching of experience, there is a mentor. Anywhere there is an individual with life lessons to impart to an audience—more often than not, just an audience of one—there is a mentor.

I think if you truly understand the meaning of mentoring, you understand it is as important as parenting; in fact, it is just like parenting. As my father often said, "There is nothing you know that you haven't learned from someone else." Everything in the world has been passed down. Every piece of knowledge is something that has been shared by someone else. If you understand it as I do, mentoring becomes your true legacy. It is the greatest inheritance you can give to others. It is why you get up every day—to teach and be taught.

BUT WHAT IS a mentor, really? What does mentoring involve, and how does it come about? When does a person become a mentor? What can an individual do to find one? And, perhaps most important, how can a person prime himself or herself to be effectively touched by the teachings of such a figure?

I think it's important to start by simply defining the concept of mentoring. The word comes from the Greek epic poem *The Odyssey*. Before Odysseus leaves for the Trojan War, he asks his old friend Mentor to look after his family and his home. When Odysseus returns home twenty years later and needs some divine assistance, the goddess Athena comes to his aid in the form of that same wise, trustworthy man, and offers Odysseus advice and counsel.

The idea to which this reliable old friend unwittingly lent his name has been passed on to us in a form not much changed from Odysseus's time. And just as Odysseus did, we often find our mentors among those close to us. In fact, once we start looking, we very often find mentors all around us.

THERE ARE A number of different kinds of mentors we can seek out—in our personal and professional lives, in our work as leaders, in our religious progress, and elsewhere. A personal mentor is an individual whose principles and values have dictated his or her decisions and actions as that person went about his or her life. These mentors can often teach us the most about effective living—about humility, contentment, interactions with family and friends, and how to keep our priorities straight in a world that often threatens to invert them. A personal mentor may encourage us as well as correct us when we find our focus shifting from the things that truly matter in living a life worthy of respect.

There is also the professional mentor, a person whose success in his or her career can be a source of practical wisdom and inspiration. This success might be measured in material gain or far-reaching influence, or in lives touched and relationships fostered. These mentors can offer a model for good business, ethical practices, and effective work habits, and they often provide the motivation we need to seize whatever opportunities come our way.

Leadership mentors are often authority figures who use their power to sculpt the lives with which they come into contact. They show us strength in their own convictions; they exhibit sound judgment in their decision making and deliberateness in their actions. Their lessons can be difficult to swallow, especially when they come in the form of discipline or perceived toughness, but their lessons stay with us for years and some-times even for a lifetime.

A mentor also can be a figure of faith—anyone from a reli-gious figure to a church leader to a quiet spirit simply devoted to God. Faith mentors can guide us to a deeper understanding, to a broader sense of purpose, or to a place of spiritual peace. They often inspire us to look beyond ourselves and develop wise discernment in our decision making and our reactions to whatever life throws at us.

There are other kinds of mentors, too, but the main thing to remember is that there is one essential difference between a hero and a mentor: A hero is someone you idolize, while a men-tor is someone you respect. A hero earns our amazement; a mentor earns our confidence. A hero takes our breath away; a mentor is given our trust. Mentors do not seek to create a new person; they simply seek to help a person become a better ver-sion of himself. Mentors are, after all, primarily concerned with teaching, and a teacher is there to inspire.

I urge everyone to seek out someone whose life inspires you and speaks to your own goals. It might be someone in your own family or someone you have never met. The important thing is that you open yourself up to be a willing student. You need to allow yourself the luxury of learning. Sometimes that might even involve swallowing a little pride, but there is nothing more valuable than learning from someone who has been there. Ad-vice, after all, is just experience without the pain of having to learn those lessons yourself.

And here's the kicker: You don't always have to agree with your mentor. In fact, some of the best learning comes from watching others' mistakes. What matters is what you do with the lessons those mentors teach you.

———————

THERE IS ANOTHER part of this equation, though. It's not enough to set about finding a mentor; it's every bit as important to concentrate on becoming one yourself. I always viewed myself as a teacher, not a coach. I wasn't just calling plays and shaping games, I was instructing young men on how to handle the ball, on how to dominate the court with all the speed they could, how to pass to teammates to make sure that the team worked as a unit. As important, I was teaching them how to share the glory, how to win and lose graciously. I sought to teach these boys about more than basketball. I wanted to teach them how to live.

During my career, I had hundreds of athletes on my teams, but I've endeavored to have many more students than that. I know that my life has been blessed with incredible opportunities, and as a result, I have a responsibility to reach out to others to share the insights, experiences, heartbreaks, exhilaration— all the lessons I've managed to accrue through the nearly one hundred years that God has given me on this planet.

We all share that same responsibility because each of us has gained a different perspective from our individual circumstances. Knowledge is nothing unless it is shared. I know that knowledge for knowledge's sake is a wonderful ideal, but in reality, it is the *transmission* of understanding that is the very basis of civilization. It's what allows human progress to move forward. If we don't pass on what we've gained, we are halting the upward reach of society, and we are denying everything that came before us that enabled *us* the luxury of learning those lessons we refuse to share. As an old saying goes, "We stand on the shoulders of giants." It is our responsibility to make our shoulders available for the next generation's climb.

Back in 1993, Charles Barkley starred in a Nike commercial where he spoke these words, punctuated with shots of him drilling with a ball: "I am not a role model. I am not paid to be a role model. I am paid to wreak havoc on the basketball court. Parents should be role models. Just because I can dunk a basketball does not mean I should raise your kids."

Barkley is absolutely right on one point: Parents should step up to their responsibilities and take charge of bringing up their children. But the rest of us have a responsibility, too, and that responsibility is to reach out to others to share our own life experiences, successes, and pitfalls. Some parents are perfect mentors, but that shouldn't stop a person from looking to other people for additional mentoring; some parents refuse to take their job seriously, and then our job as mentors becomes even more important. Do any of us really have a choice as to whether a child looks up to us? Do we have any control over another person's choice to look to model themselves after our own lives? The fact is that we all possess the ability to mentor, but to fully realize that potential, we need to recognize what gives us that strength and what we have to offer to others.

The English teacher side of me shows a bit when I point out that the word "mentor" is both a verb and a noun. It is simultaneously something you do and something you are. The first definition is one you can control; the second one isn't. In other words, you can make a conscious decision to sit down with someone and share wisdom, experience, and encouragement. That is mentoring. However, you also can become a mentor whenever someone chooses to learn from you. You may never have met; your lives may never intersect; nevertheless, you can become a source of guidance and inspiration for another person. That's being a mentor.

THERE ARE SEVEN mentors who had an enormous role in shaping my own life. These individuals have inspired me in more ways than I can count. Some are remarkable world figures; others are quiet persons of dignity who never saw their names in the newspaper, let alone a history book. But together, these mentors shaped my life into one that was equipped to shape the lives of others. I look to these figures for guidance, and I owe my various successes to them. Collectively, my mentors challenged me to be better and encouraged me to persevere.

The first mentor on my list is my father, Joshua Wooden. His life was a study in contentment and humility—two qualities that are sadly lacking in today's society.

The second is Earl Warriner, my elementary school principal and earliest basketball coach, a man who insisted on discipline and responsibility with such kind authority that I have never forgotten the lessons he taught.

My high school coach, Glenn Curtis, is next. He showed me that coaching is really just teaching, and this philosophy changed my outlook on everything.

Then there is Piggy Lambert, my coach at Purdue, who stressed the team above the individual. This mind-set taught me about more than the game of basketball; it taught me selflessness and the importance of relationships.

Mother Teresa is one mentor I never met, but value no less because of it. She embodied Piggy Lambert's emphasis on selflessness in a whole new way, and coupled it with conviction, faith, and persistence. She truly lived her life for others and showed consideration to everyone she met, whether she agreed with them or not. Her example has taught me more patience and peace than I ever imagined possible.

Abraham Lincoln is a similar kind of mentor. I obviously never met him, but my personal library contains nearly four dozen books about his life (I have a similar number about Mother Teresa). Lincoln's cool-headedness in the midst of the country's greatest internal trial exhibited wisdom, and the gentle way in which he interacted with those around him demonstrated compassion. I can think of no two attributes more essential than these in a good leader.

There is no doubt that Mother Teresa and Abraham Lincoln were extraordinary human beings. But they also should remind us that anyone can look to anyone else and learn a lesson—even if it's a basketball coach learning from a nun and a statesman!

And finally there is my wife, Nellie. She taught me more about love, trust, forgiveness, and patience than any individual I have ever known. As I watched her raise our children into amazing adults; as I watched her follow my career around the country, always trusting that I would make the best decision for our family; as I listened to her words of comfort and encouragement during the difficult periods; as she met the exciting times with enthusiasm and humility, I was being mentored. I didn't necessarily recognize it as such, but now that her gentle voice and loving spirit are gone, I understand now that very much of who I am I owe to that incredible woman and tremendous mentor.

I HOPE THAT through this book, we can all be challenged, all be taught how to become one of those life-changing teachers. I hope that when we're done, we can be open both to the mentoring experience and to accepting the responsibility of becoming a mentor.

CHAPTER 2

Joshua Wooden

"THERE IS NOTHING YOU KNOW that you haven't learned from someone else." My father used to repeat that to my three brothers and me while we were growing up on a struggling Indiana farm in the 1920s. I didn't really appreciate it at the time, but now I realize he was reminding us that life is a learning opportunity and that lessons are constantly being taught all around us. I think he also was reminding us to always be thankful for each lesson an individual offers, wittingly or unwittingly, because those lessons become a kind of borrowed experience.

By most people's standards, the experiences of Joshua Wooden are hardly worth noting. In fact, for a lot of people he might have represented a lesson in what *not* to do: He never got excited, he never fought back, and he never had much material wealth to show for all of his hard work. He lost his farm and his livelihood but he never lost his temper; he valued gentleness above all, but he gave no value to a gentleman over anyone else; he was humble and he was proud; he lived simply but was incredibly complex. And as I watched him through the dramatic struggles and quiet triumphs of his life, I came to appreciate what a remarkable man and mentor my father truly was.

Some of my earliest and happiest memories involve the nightly ritual in which my father would read to us from the Bible and from classic English poets—he especially loved poetry. In those early years our home was simple, without indoor plumbing or electric light. We were poor; there was no question about that. But we never felt poor, because of the contentedness with which my parents lived their lives. To my father, being able to provide for his family with his own hands and having the joy of a good book were the greatest luxuries he could imagine. He never dwelled on what he could not provide for us. Instead, he invested his time in developing the character of his four rowdy, head-strong boys: Maurice, myself, Danny, and Billy.

It couldn't have been an easy task, but my father never opted for the easy way out. He believed in doing things the right way and accepted no excuses for a job left unfinished. His convictions are what stand out the most to me; he was truer to them than most men might think possible. But my father was not like most men. In fact, he was unlike any man I have ever known or am likely to ever meet. His life was the earliest and most significant example I ever had of how to be a person of principle, persistence, and compassion—three characteristics that became my guideposts for teaching, both in the classroom and on the court.

I don't recall the moment when I realized what a tremendous mentor I had in my father, but I do remember the event that demonstrated to me how very seriously he took that role. I've talked before about the graduation gift my father gave to each of his sons when we completed grade school: a two-dollar bill, and a small card with a poem on one side and seven rules for living on the other:

1. Be true to yourself.
2. Make each day your masterpiece.
3. Help others.
4. Drink deeply from good books.
5. Make friendship a fine art.
6. Build a shelter against a rainy day.
7. Pray for guidance and give thanks for your blessings every day.

Some people might not understand why something so small has proven to be so monumentally important to me over the years, but it was so much more than just a simple present. My father gave me the gift of advice, the gift of mentorship.

The way he lived his life already supplied my brothers and me with a lifetime of lessons on being a better person, but when he handed me that card inscribed with the seven points he thought were the most valuable, he opened up a world to me by making me realize the importance of sharing experience with others. I suddenly realized that advice was not trying to voice one's opinion, but rather, a valuable tool for strengthening the listener and giving him a leg up in his own situation. What an amazing gift—to be able to give someone knowledge from experience!

As the years went on and I read and reread that card, it became increasingly important to me because I could see others around me struggling with the very situations or emotions my father had warned me against. The lessons he taught gave me a different outlook on life. By sharing what he knew to be true, he gave me an advantage far beyond any that money could have bought.

Nowadays, parents are often too concerned with having their children like them than they are with having their children respect them. Parents need to be parents, not friends, to their children. I believe that my father's graduation gift was a perfect illustration of effective parenting—which is to say, effective mentoring. By entrusting me with the most important wisdom he had collected throughout his years, he was letting me know that I was now a young man and needed to begin to think of myself in those terms, rather than as a child. At the same time, that card was a reminder that I still had things to learn, and he still had things to teach me. I recognized that he remained the head of our household and that his experience was something I should trust, respect, and learn from. My father's main concern was caring for his family, which included raising his children to be the best men they could possibly be.

My father used the immediate to prepare us for the future. That is what effective teachers do—they recognize where you are, and utilize their own knowledge to prepare you for what lies ahead. I don't think it's any coincidence that all four of us boys ended up becoming classroom teachers. A love for learning—whether it was from books or from life—surrounded us from our earliest days, as did a sense of peace that can only stem from true contentedness. These were the lessons my father passed on to his sons.

MY FATHER'S LOVE was nowhere more apparent than in how he treated my mother. From watching the respect that they had for one another, I learned the true meaning of my father's favorite quote from Abraham Lincoln: "The best thing a father can do for his children is to love their mother."

If children grow up in an atmosphere of respect and appreciation between their parents, they will conduct the relationships in their lives on similar terms. After all, our parents are almost universally the first adults with whom we have any long-term contact. Their behavior first indicates to us how people should act toward one another.

My parents married young (my father was twenty, my mother sixteen), but that wasn't exceptional in those days. They had known each other's families growing up, respected each other's character and faith, and were committed to creating a loving home for whatever children God might bring their way. They were never overly affectionate toward each other—not in front of us kids, anyway—but they interacted with one another in a sort of kindness that spoke their love loud and clear.

I have written and talked a great deal during my long career about my father's tremendous influence on my life, but have neglected to say much about my mother. That is a great oversight, as she was an incredible woman who managed a household with none of the modern conveniences and suffered the loss of both her daughters within a year of one another— Cordelia, who was born between my older brother Maurice and myself, died of diphtheria when she was two; and there was a baby girl who died at birth and was never named. And yet Mother never once complained, or lost her faith, or showed any kind of self-pity. Instead, she poured herself into the lives of her surviving children with a fierce devotion that celebrated her love for us all.

If a neighbor happened to remark, "Johnny played a great game of basketball last week," she would thank them for the praise then add, "And Billy just earned full marks on his history test today." She never tried to take away from the success of any one of us, but wanted to make sure that all of her children were honored equally. If one of us boys had earned special honor, she would dedicate a little extra attention to the other ones to make sure we understood that her love had nothing to do with our accomplishments. She celebrated alongside us, but she also made sure that her affection was completely separate from that, too. Our value to her was because of who we were, not what we did.

This was a lesson I carried with me as I began to teach basketball. When one of my players scored, he knew he was supposed to point to the teammate who had passed him the ball or made the block that allowed that basket to happen. It wasn't about deflecting praise, but about sharing it with everyone who was working hard as a part of the team.

My brothers and I rarely argued; we felt strongly that we were all part of the same team and tried to act accordingly. Maurice was certainly capable of arguing—his nickname in town was "Cat," because there was a boy at school with whom he argued "like cats and dogs." But that kind of fighting never came home. We never felt our parents favored one child over another, never allowed jealousy or resentment from one brother's success to overshadow the rest of us. Mother saw to that.

Ultimately, though, it really is my father from whom I learned more, perhaps because I spent more time with him pushing a plow or driving a team of horses out in the fields than in the house with Mother. Even my respect and love for her was influenced by the tender care and devotion that my father showed her every day. Perhaps it would be fair to say that the loving home she created established the perfect backdrop for the lessons my father would teach me.

MY FATHER TRULY had a love for every living creature, and it was apparent in the way he worked with both animals and people. There was a time when we were working at the local gravel pit and a team of horses was struggling with the load. Their driver was whipping them and hollering and raising a ruckus, but my father stepped up to the team and spoke to them quietly, then grasped the bridle and calmly led them forward. It was an incredible reminder that gentleness can fix in a moment what an hour of shouting fails to achieve.

His gentleness affected the way he interacted with other people as well. It didn't matter if they were rich or poor, well dressed or in dirty work clothes; my father treated everyone with respect. Whatever your job or title or social status, he spoke with the same quiet tone, the same level of interest, and the same genuine concern in every conversation he had. It wasn't that he avoided emotion; it was that he felt the same tremendous compassion for everyone he met. He certainly didn't like everyone or approve of their choices, but he never allowed that to affect the regard he showed for them with the gentleness of his interactions.

"Remember this," he used to say to us. "You're as good as anybody. But never forget you're no better than anybody, either." He stressed the balance between pride in oneself and humility of spirit. "Don't look down on anybody. *Don't look down on them*," he'd say. I remember his exact words because his adherence to them never wavered.

My father's spirit of gentleness came to be one of the trademarks of my coaching. He never yelled, never grew angry, and treated everyone with respect. In interviews, I was inevitably asked about why I sat on the bench with a rolled-up program in my hand rather than pacing the sidelines, hollering out directions to the players and objections to the referees.

The answer to that is simple: I did what my father would have done.

Before each game I would tell my players, "I've done *my* job coaching you this past week, now get out there and do yours." I couldn't see the point in getting excited and angry and all riled up the way many other coaches did during play. To me, that conveyed a sense of unease to my players by indicating that I didn't trust them to get the job done. I think it's like my father with those horses at the gravel pit—a few quiet words of assurance and a gentle, confident hand were much more effective in helping them to move than shouting and excitability. And just like those scared, frustrated horses, my players responded by delivering the job that needed doing.

But my father's example came into my teaching long before we ever hit the court. In fact, we would always hold a team meeting a few weeks before the start of the season and I would tell my players, "Now, I'm not going to treat you all the same, I don't like you all the same, you don't like each other all the same, don't like me all the same. I hope I will be strong enough to not permit my personal likes or dislikes to have any bearing on how I get you to play. I know I will love you all the same. I won't like you all the same, but I'll love you all the same." That was the promise I made to them, and I kept it.

I gave that same speech every year, pretty much word for word. That didn't mean it wasn't from the heart—quite the opposite, actually. I had thought about it long enough that I had tweaked it to exactly the kind of language and tone I wanted my players to hear from me.

I had to be honest with my players—there were going to be times I didn't like them or didn't like what they did. That's just a reality of human existence; there will be people with whom you click better than others. But I wanted them to know I loved them, and a poor choice or poor playing or poor attitude would never take away my love. They were not just players to me; that was incidental. They were individuals first, and that was the source of their value.

I think that kind of assurance at the start of every season was paramount in creating the right dynamic—between myself and the players, and from one teammate to another. I really wanted to stress the importance of their personal lives away from the court, so they did not derive their sense of worth from how they played from one game to the next. Sure, your self-esteem or confidence might be a little shaken after a bad game, but it doesn't lessen your importance as a person.

I tried to bring that philosophy to the way I interacted with my coaching staff, too. As my father reminded me more than once, "Great leaders give credit to others and accept the blame themselves." If one of my assistant coaches made a suggestion that we decided to implement, I would make sure to praise him for his foresight in the press conference afterward. But if one made a suggestion that didn't prove to be as successful, I accepted the blame myself rather than pinning it on the assistant. After all, as the head coach, I had decided to go forward with it. I found that this was the most effective way to keep my assistant coaches feeling engaged with the game, willing to make suggestions, and ready to contribute to the betterment of the team.

It worked with my players, too. I would never publicly criticize a player for poor performance. Even in moments of extreme frustration, I would check myself because it just didn't seem right—because it didn't seem like something my father would have done. And I'm proud to say that to the best of my knowledge, I never did slip up in that regard.

My father refused to speak an unkind word against anyone. I know—I tried to get him to do it. My older brother Maurice especially liked the game. He would start a conversation and then ask my father for his reaction or response, but my father knew that we were trying to lure him into a slipup, so he would just laugh and refuse to take the bait. It was amazing; but growing up under such a strong example of that, I found that it inherently became part of my own character.

That's one of the important things about mentoring that I believe is often overlooked: Some lessons are learned more subconsciously than consciously. There are things I learned from watching my father that I purposely tried to copy in my own life. But other things I found were just kind of absorbed and became a part of my thinking and reactions without my really thinking much about them.

I admired my father's refusal to speak badly about others, but I don't think I necessarily set out to make that a rule for myself. I imagine I considered that to be too lofty a goal. Yet as time went on, I found it was a practice that had etched itself onto my soul so that if I ever slipped up on that matter, I felt pain rather than satisfaction.

Looking back, it seems clear that my father's gentleness extended from his incredible peace of mind. He understood the importance of confidence and contentment in one's own self, and that radiated from him and touched whoever or whatever might be around. Colts that were bucking and kicking so wildly that no one could get close to them would be calmed in just a few minutes once my father entered the pen and spoke to them with his strong but gentle voice. Dogs that terrified me would lick my father's hand when he approached. His peace of mind was infectious. You couldn't help but feel at ease when my father was in the room because absolute serenity just seemed to follow him. It's impossible to teach that kind of grace because it comes from true contentment from the depth of the soul. It can only be obtained by being in its presence and absorbing it yourself.

That, I believe, is the real value of surrounding oneself with people of strong character. They not only give us an opportunity to study and learn from their lives and habits, they also make us better simply by their proximity, a kind of learning by osmosis.

For example, whenever I walked into the locker room, if there was a piece of trash on the floor, I'd drop it into the trash can. If there was a towel left out, I'd pick it up and bring it to the laundry bin. I realized pretty quickly that whenever my players would see me do this, they'd immediately spring to action, too, paying attention to anything they might have dropped or saying, "I've got it, Coach!" and depositing the towel where it needed to go.

I'm proud to say that in the course of my career I received many, many letters from maintenance staff and athletic directors informing me that my team left the visitors' locker cleaner than any other team. I really don't think the players went in there thinking, "Let's make sure we clean up so Coach won't get on our case." I think it came naturally to them because they saw me do it out of habit.

It was a very minor thing—picking up after ourselves—but it said something significant to those who had to come behind us and clean up. It made their job a little easier, which showed respect and consideration for them. Even simple consideration can be contagious—and that's mentoring, too.

In December 2008, the *British Medical Journal* published a study that confirmed what many of us have known for a long time: Happiness actually spreads through social interactions and connections. When the people around a person are positive, cheerful, engaged, and contented, the feelings of that individual are likely to reflect those same emotions. In other words, you are directly affected by the behavior of those around you, and your example can influence the attitude and behavior of others.

And I don't think the link has to be as direct as close friends and family, either. Think about all of the complex networks we engage in every day, from the people we see at the store to the customer service agent we talk to on the phone. A smile for the busy waitress, an encouraging word to the stressed-out mother with a screaming toddler, patience with the technical-support guy as he tries to answer your question—any of these can make a difference in that person's day. And if the person behind you in line sees you act kindly toward the cashier, he or she will be more inclined to do the same. It was wonderful to see the phenomenon of contagious happiness confirmed by science, but I already knew it was true. I'd seen my father's influence and felt it myself.

It would be wrong, however, to assume that being mentored is always as simple as absorbing a positive example. Sometimes the opportunity for mentoring comes from passing on what one has gained from learning an incredibly painful lesson.

While I was still in high school, my father decided to invest in some hogs for our farm. He felt that by diversifying the scope of our agriculture, we would be able to have more security in case one of the other aspects of our farm failed. Hogs were not cheap, so he had to take out a mortgage to pay for them. It was a risk, but my father knew that there was no amount of hard work he was unwilling to do, so he felt he could guarantee the risk by the work of his own two hands.

What he could not anticipate, though, was the failure of others. He purchased a batch of vaccinations for the herd, which was necessary to keep them healthy while we raised them. But the vaccinations were bad, and the entire stock died. All of our hogs were wiped out, and that same season, a drought hit the crops. My father was left with a struggling farm and a large mortgage, and the bank reclaimed it all.

Suddenly he was a man who had lost his life's work and the family land. And yet without a single word against the man who had sold him the bad serum, he packed up the family and moved us to the nearby town of Martinsville, where he accepted a job as a masseur in one of the hot springs sanitariums there.

I know his spirit was absolutely crushed by what had happened and his heart ached for what had been lost, yet he lived by the advice he had always given to his sons whenever we'd fuss about something beyond our control: "Don't whine, don't complain, don't make excuses. Just do the best you can. Nobody can do more than that."

He refused to dwell on mistakes or assign blame. Instead, he sought to rejoice in making the best he possibly could out of what he was given. It was in that lesson, I believe, that my own personal definition of success began to take shape years before I ever wrote it down: "Success is peace of mind, which is a direct result of self-satisfaction in knowing you made the effort to become the best of which you are capable."

And even in the midst of what some people might consider a humiliating circumstance, my father never let his circumstances change him for the worse. He always sought to improve his mind, even if his situation was beyond his control.

For example, he was well known in our community as the finest checker player around. He could outmaneuver people three plays ahead of where they were. One day, a world-class chess player came to the hot springs on a visit and started asking around the sanitarium if anyone there played chess. The answer he received over and over was, "No, but Joshua Wooden will play a game of checkers like you've never seen."

They did end up playing a number of games of checkers during the man's stay, and I don't recall who won more games, but by the end of the visit, my father had asked that man to teach him how to play chess. He knew he probably wouldn't have anyone to play against in town, but my father never let a learning opportunity pass him by. He ended up teaching a lot of other people in Martinsville how to play chess, too, all thanks to his perpetual openness to understanding more, asking questions, and encouraging people to share their talents, experiences, and expertise with him.

That attitude of openness is the bedrock of mentoring, I believe. You can be a mentor—my father certainly was—but you must still be receptive to learning yourself, to being mentored. Maybe learning chess seems like a silly thing to talk about in terms of teaching life lessons, but I think it represents much more than just a way to pass the time. Chess is a game of strategy and observation. You have to keep your eye always on your opponent, absorbing each of his or her moves and allowing them to influence your decision making and battle plan. In a lot of ways, that's akin to mentoring: closely watching those around you and learning from their mistakes and victories, incorporating those lessons into your own choices—and knowing that someone is always watching you as well.

THERE IS A famous quote attributed to Mark Twain: "When I was a boy of fourteen, my father was so ignorant I could hardly stand to have the old man around. But when I got to be twenty-one, I was astonished at how much the old man had learned in seven years."

When I was younger, I didn't understand why my father was the way he was. Why didn't he ever seem to get angry? Why wouldn't he strike back at people who had done him wrong? Why was he always making so much time for other people? By the world's standards, he was a failure: a farmer who couldn't farm, a man of no real importance.

As I grew to be a man, I slowly began not only to understand how incredibly wise my father was, but also to appreciate the various ways he had taught me: by offering advice and counsel in difficult situations, by providing a strong example, and by giving me a tangible reminder of his wisdom on a tiny little paper card. Some people might dismiss him as having not been of much consequence himself, but the legacy he left was immeasurable.

He showed me love, kindness, gentleness, responsibility, and peace of mind. He mentored me with lessons, with actions, and with words so that long before I ever set foot in my first classroom, I already knew both how to learn and how to teach. I can think of no greater lesson than that.

. . . .

CHAPTER 3

Earl Warriner

I have always felt that there is a special relationship between a coach and his or her athletes. Because of the amount of time spent together and the sheer physical exhaustion that results from giving maximum effort in practice or in a game, there isn't room for pretense or inhibitions or ceremony or posturing. Coaches and players interact in a way that is probably more honest and frank than almost any other relationship in a young person's life.

But the lessons taught are more than athletic skills or game strategy. Coaches teach athletes their own philosophies and worldviews; and when those players go on to become professional athletes, coaches, or dedicated fans, the philosophies they carry with them affect the future direction and culture of the entire sport.

In the following three chapters, I will be discussing the significance of three coaches whose influence changed my playing and my life. They didn't just teach me skills; they also taught me how to teach.

IN THE FOYER OF MY CONDOMINIUM in Encino, California, hanging on the wall to the right as you walk in, is a beautiful oil painting of a country cabin nestled in the woods. Clearly the product of talented hands, it was the gift of a woman named Martha, the granddaughter of one of my earliest and most influential mentors. That painting hangs by the doorway to remind me every time I get ready to leave the house of the wisdom, values, and patience of one extraordinary person who, more than ninety years ago, began to change the way I live my daily life—a man who mentors me still today.

Besides my father, the first man whose example really stood out to me was a stern, no-nonsense figure who loomed large over my grade school years. His name was Earl Warriner, and he was the principal and basketball coach at our little country grade school on the outskirts of Martinsville, Indiana.

We were all a little terrified of him—he was a strict disciplinarian and taskmaster, a gifted athlete with unshakable values—but I think we all loved him for the same reasons. He represented everything that elicits wonder and respect from school-age boys. From this experience I learned that no one is too young to be mentored, and that we all have the potential to be mentors with every decision we make.

PERHAPS MY MOST prominent recollection of Mr. Warriner is one people seem to love to tell, and hear me tell, and that is "The Star-Spangled Banner" episode. Whenever I recount the story, everyone seems to get a real laugh out of it; I guess the image of a calm, put-together college coach getting a switch to the bottom as a defiant child really is funny. But there is a reason that the story is such an important one in my life.

It all started when four of my teammates and I—we were about nine or ten at the time—decided that we were too cool to sing the national anthem with the rest of the school in the morning assembly. I'm not sure why we found this act of childish rebellion so powerfully attractive, but we did, and Mr. Warriner decided to repay childish behavior with childish punishment. He called all of our parents to inform them of his plans for us; and when the next morning came and we refused to sing again, he called us out in front of the entire school and then took us to another room, where he had switches ready. He looked at us sternly and said, "Are you going to sing today?" We saw those switches and we knew what was coming, but we were stubborn boys, and the thrill of our daring must have gone to our heads. We said no.

Then he marched us back out in front of the whole assembly—close to a hundred children. One by one he went down the line and asked each of us again, "Are you going to sing today?" One by one we refused a second time, and the switches came out to do their job. That's when one of our number finally said, "Okay, I'll sing!" But Mr. Warriner knew that the boy had been as much of a culprit as the rest of us and replied, "We'll see about that." And the switch came down. Another boy had worn two pairs of pants in anticipation of what we knew must be coming. Mr. Warriner made him take the top pair off, so that his punishment would sting as much as the rest of ours.

When I arrived home that evening, my mother was a little upset about what had taken place. She seemed to think that Mr. Warriner had been too harsh with his punishment. But she respected his position as the principal of the school, and she knew that I had misbehaved. What I think really surprised her was that I wasn't mad at him. I liked him before the incident, and I liked him even more afterward. We'd had it coming with the way we were challenging him, and he didn't back down from that.

From that one rather silly instance from my childhood, I

was able to glean a lot of very valuable lessons. First, it was clear that Mr. Warriner placed a great value on the national anthem and believed in the importance of sharing that with the students in his charge. He had a value system that was clearly defined, and respect was at the top of his list. Mr. Warriner didn't discipline us because we refused to sing "The Star-Spangled Banner." He disciplined us because we were defying him.

This was the same lesson I would try to pass on to Bill Walton years later, as he was part of the protests against the Vietnam War that were occurring around campus. I recognized his right to protest—that is one of the things that makes America great. But when I questioned his decision to be part of a group that would lie down in the middle of the road to block traffic so that people couldn't get to work, I wanted him to understand that his patriotism should challenge ideas, not disrespect people. That is an important difference, and Mr. Warriner first put me on the path to recognizing it.

The second lesson I took from the whole incident was that Mr. Warriner held his players to a higher standard because we represented the school. Not only did that make us ambassadors of our town at the other schools in neighboring areas, but it also meant that in the complex social hierarchy of grade school politics, we were near the top of the heap and our behavior would affect the behavior of our peers.

As a coach myself, I implemented this same approach. I wanted my players to represent themselves and their school in the best possible light. What mattered to me was not just the way the school we represented was perceived by fans, rivals, and the media; it also mattered that professors and students closer to home had positive interactions with my players. I wanted my students to be responsible, trustworthy, and never to expect special treatment because of the jersey they wore.

When Mr. Warriner humbled us in front of the school, he reminded our classmates (and especially the five of us boys) that we were not above the rules.

While mentoring is usually about building someone up, it can occasionally be about taking someone down a notch or two, too—provided the dressing down is done with that person's best interest at heart and that it stems from love. I never doubted that Mr. Warriner loved us. He wasn't trying to embarrass us to make himself look tough; he was trying to hold us accountable for our choices and to keep us on the right path by not allowing us to ever think too much of ourselves.

The third lesson, which lasted far longer than my stinging bottom, was that Mr. Warriner had given us a chance to change our behavior. By taking us aside and showing us the switches in the other room, he gave us a chance to reconsider our actions and to recant privately. I respected that, and later on I would always try to follow his example with my players by taking them aside and speaking to them privately if there was an issue I felt needed attention. If there is a problem, it should be addressed early on, but it also should be addressed quietly.

This not only allows the individual a chance to listen to the criticism and think about how to resolve the matter, but it often also creates a bond between the teacher and the student. There is an understanding that is forged and an appreciation for the private correction. No one likes to be called out in front of his or her friends. Humiliation is not the same thing as correction: One attacks the person; the other attacks the problem.

But once Mr. Warriner realized that our egos were too big for us to back down, he took us in front of the school and made it clear that such behavior was not to be tolerated. This was his last resort, not his first action. That was an important lesson for me. It showed me that he was acting in a careful, measured way rather than with a knee-jerk response of anger. A coach's emotions have no place on the court. Discipline applied fairly and effectively rarely needs to be repeated.

The last, and perhaps most important lesson in mentoring I learned from Mr. Warriner that day was that consistency is the key to respect. He did not back down, nor did he change his mind. He believed that young men should act in a respectful manner, and he pursued the course of action he saw as necessary to uphold that principle. He held us to a standard, and he expected us to hold ourselves to it as well. When our behavior exhibited less character than it should, he carefully and deliberately took steps to correct it, and the fact that my friend wore two pairs of pants shows that we knew what to expect.

Consistency is essential. You have to make sure that your students know what is expected of them and what the consequences will be if those expectations are not met. My players knew that the team bus left precisely at the time I said it would. They knew what behaviors would be tolerated (politeness) and what would not (any form of disrespect toward the other team, its staff, its facilities, or its fans), and they knew that the rules wouldn't change.

Hand in hand with consistency come honesty and trust. When a teacher or a coach or any kind of mentor is consistent in his or her principles, it creates trust between the mentor and the people he or she is mentoring. I always tried to keep this in mind when I gave recruiting talks to prospective players. If a player was interested in UCLA—I was never a coach who favored aggressive recruiting—I would talk with him honestly and frankly about what might be in store for him if he decided on my school.

I never tried to talk a student into coming to UCLA. I tried to show him what was there and what to expect, and I never told him he was going to play; I told him he would have the *opportunity* to play, and if he was good enough, then he'd be able to.

Rosy forecasts during the "courtship" of a player can only lead to disappointment and distrust if anything fails to meet that student's expectations.

Instead, I would tell each student that if he did choose to attend UCLA—and I hoped he would—that he would be very unhappy his first year. "You're going to be away from home and your parents and all the things you've known for a number of years," I'd explain. "It's going to be very different academically and you're going to wish you had gone someplace else. But let me tell you this: If you had gone someplace else, it would be the same thing and you'd wonder what would have happened if you'd gone to UCLA. So there you go. Think it over."

Certainly it was a less elaborate recruiting speech than they received at many other universities, but it was very effective, I believe, because it started the coach-player relationship on a note of honesty.

That same level of honesty is required of a mentor. You have to be willing to identify a need, weakness, or even an unpleasant reality but also assure your mentee that you're going to help him or her overcome it. The frankness builds trust, while the positive action you take builds character. As Mr. Warriner had shown me years before, a man of his word will be a more effective leader than a man who derives his power from fear, empty promises, or inconsistent policies. Honesty usually leads to respect, and respect can be the key to really reaching a person and changing his or her life. I've always been proud of the recruiting classes that chose to come to UCLA, and I've always been thankful to the man who taught me how to be a respected administrator.

MR. WARRINER'S VALUES were an inseparable part of who he was. He lived them unwaveringly, and they dictated his every relationship, every interaction, and every lesson. Perhaps nothing illustrates this more clearly than another instance, when little headstrong Johnny Wooden, this time about thirteen years old, screwed up and Coach Warriner stepped in with a lesson that would change my life.

I had forgotten my uniform and did not want to run the mile or so back to our farm to retrieve it before that afternoon's basketball game. Besides, I was the best player on our team—I was sure there was no way Coach was going to bench me. I was wrong.

When it became clear that I would not be allowed to play without the uniform, I talked a teammate into going home to fetch it for me. After all, I was the star, right? Why shouldn't I be allowed to ask a favor or two from the benchwarmers? With that attitude, it's no wonder that the game started without me in it. When I tried to reason with Coach, pleading with him to let me play because it was clear we were outmatched with our new starting lineup, he told me very simply, "Johnny, there are some things more important than winning."

Some things more important than winning? Not many coaches could convince a thirteen-year-old boy to believe that. But as I sat miserably on the bench, watching my team fall farther and farther behind, I started to realize that maybe Coach Warriner was right. Maybe I did need to be taken down a notch or two. As I grew up and that experience stayed with me, I really came to appreciate its significance. The life lessons in responsibility and humility that I needed to learn trumped a hatch mark in the loss column of a grade school–league record book. And at the start of the second half, Coach let me in the game.

That may seem contrary to what I just said above about the importance of consistency, but I think that what my coach was showing me was that while there was a lesson to be learned, it is equally important to make the punishment fit the crime, and not to be so focused on your toughness that you lose sight of the bigger issue and the person you're supposed to be teaching.

Looking back on my time at UCLA, maybe I could have been a little more lenient about some of my requirements about long hair or facial hair. My players could not sport a hairstyle that touched their collars, and they had to be clean-shaven. (Given that I was coaching in the 1960s and 1970s, this was really a tall order.) The players all complied—eventually—because they knew my rules. But really, as long as my players were well groomed and respectful, I guess it didn't matter what they chose to do with their hair.

It's essential for an effective teacher to remain open-minded when it comes to punishment. While consistency is very important, so is showing a little mercy when it is clear that the lesson has gotten through—like with Coach Warriner letting me off the bench after halftime.

Even more important, though, is flexibility when special circumstances arise. Absolutes are important, but understanding can be even more so. There is one instance in particular when I truly regret having stuck to my guns. It was in one of my first years of teaching, when I was still at the high school level. I had a strict rule about smoking: Absolutely no one could smoke during the basketball season.

I probably should add that I was a smoker myself after picking it up while in the Navy, but I would quit before the start of the season every year, and start up again after it ended. I continued this pattern for several years before I finally decided that this practice was silly and the habit was pointless, and I gave up smoking for good.

Anyway, there was a young man named Parsons Howell, and when he was caught smoking, I told him that he was going to be kicked off the team. He begged me not to do it and promised that he would not light up again during the season. He was struggling in life, I could tell, and basketball was the one thing that kept him centered. But still, I refused to budge. In my mind at that time, rules were rules, and that was all there was to it. Not long afterward, he dropped out of high school. I never learned what happened to him.

I have always regretted that decision. What I should have done was extend to him the same courtesy that Mr. Warriner had extended to me: a second chance.

Ultimately, I think today's youth are exactly the same as youth were fifty years ago and the same as fifty years before that and the same as youth will be fifty years from now. It is society that has changed, and children are just trying to find their place in it. But children almost universally are also looking for loving correction. I know that may sound a little crazy: What child looks forward to discipline?

I look around now and see that many parents aren't concerned with disciplining their children, or are afraid to try to exercise any authority over them. What they don't realize is that they are damaging their children by denying them the most precious gift of all: a stable foundation that teaches them how to function in society.

One of the reasons why men like my father and my coaches stand out so strongly in my mind is because they understood the importance of correction. It may seem a little counterintuitive that the boys of my school all looked up to our principal as a larger-than-life figure, but it's because Mr. Warriner was truly concerned about preparing us to be men of responsibility and character. We didn't necessarily understand all of that at the time, but we could clearly see his concern, his fairness, and his patience. He was not afraid of his role as an authority figure.

THERE WERE PLENTY of other lessons that Earl Warriner taught his students. He played baseball in the summers, with a number of other men from town. They'd take on semipro teams that would roll through on barnstorming tours. That, of course, made him a veritable superhero to all the boys in town. The tall, almost austere figure from school became a boy again out on the diamond, catching pop flies and sliding into bases.

The one thing I remember that we all commented on as we walked home dissecting each play at the conclusion of every game was that Mr. Warriner never gave up. He never stopped giving the game his all. Even when they were way behind, he hustled to every catch, ran full-bore to every base, and swung with all his might.

For us, watching our principal take the field with guys who might someday play in the majors was like knowing a celebrity. We were so proud of him and cheered him on as loudly as we could. And even in the summer heat, in the middle of a game that was probably his retreat from the stresses of running a school and keeping students in line, he played hard and he played to the end.

But to this day, I believe that he didn't play with that level of drive merely because it was how he approached everything (though I know that was certainly true). I believe he was keenly aware of the young eyes watching him; and even when he was out on the field instead of in the schoolhouse, he was commit-ted to teaching us how to live. Earl Warriner was a teacher through and through. He made the world his classroom and taught us whenever he had the opportunity. It wasn't always reading or math or history. He taught us all kinds of lessons. He felt it was his responsibility.

It's our responsibility, too. Everyone, regardless of their position or their job or their college degree or professional li-censure, is a teacher in some form or another. You can't be a teacher to everyone, but there always is someone you can reach with your life. Example is the best teacher. It's the key. And it's something we all can do.

I WISH I could close this chapter by saying that when I came home from college, Mr. Warriner was there to greet me, and we laughed about the old times in his familiar office—but I can't. Some years after I left his school, the son of a very prominent man in town caused some pretty bad trouble at the school. The father made it very clear to Mr. Warriner that his son was not to be disciplined. Mr. Warriner, of course, did not back down. "He will be punished," he calmly replied.

"Then you won't be principal!" the angry father promised. He was a powerful, influential man who knew how to gain alliances and manipulate people to get what he wanted.

When Mr. Warriner realized that he was being forced to choose between his principles and his job, he knew that there was no choice to be made. He promptly handed in his resignation to the school board, and left the little grade school he had lovingly developed over many, many years.

I don't know where he went after that; he was hired by a school system somewhere else, I suppose. It wasn't until years later that I was able to reconnect with his family, a reunion that resulted in the wonderful painting now hanging in my foyer. His daughter had heard me speak about my deep respect for her father and sent it to me to show how much my affection for him meant to her. He truly was a wonderful man, and it still strikes me as such a tragedy that a man of conviction and solid values would be punished for standing by them.

But even in his departure from the school and the students he loved so well, Mr. Warriner was teaching an important life lesson: There is nothing more important than a person's principles. And like the mentor he always was, he lived by his own.

CHAPTER 4

Glenn Curtis

IN NEW YORK AND CHICAGO, THE 1920S were marked by loud, boisterous nights filled with people wearing flashy clothes and dropping big dollars at speakeasies. In small towns in Indiana, those same nights were passed in an even noisier way: with teenagers in sneakers and gym shorts darting up and down the glossy oak floors of local gymnasiums.

When I first beheld the Martinsville High School gymnasium—home to the Artesians—it was the most awe-inspiring structure I had ever laid eyes on. Being a farm boy and living in the country, I rarely saw a large assembly of people anywhere except at church. You couldn't have convinced me through any application of rhetoric or logic that the Martinsville High School gym wasn't bigger than Madison Square Garden.

There were fifty-five hundred or so seats, and even though there weren't fifty-five hundred people in the entire town of Martinsville, it didn't matter—those seats were always filled. People piled in from every little farming community and unincorporated village. Some came in wagons or on horseback. Others walked. A few rich people even drove automobiles. And the thing was, it wasn't like this just a few nights of the season for the "big games." Every game was a big game.

And the grand marshal of it all was a remarkable man who patiently prepared his team to focus on the game—not the showmanship of playing the crowd, not the spectacle of the arena—but the fundamentals of dribbling and shooting, and the importance of teamwork. Glenn Curtis, one of the finest high school coaches Indiana has ever known, transformed the huge Martinsville High School gym into a private classroom as he showed his team that coaching is really just teaching, and mentoring is sometimes just a matter of being who you are.

MR. CURTIS BELIEVED in the fundamentals. He believed that you can't have a good basketball game without a good basketball team, you can't have a good team without good players, you can't have good players without good skills, and you can't have good skills without good practice. He wasn't concerned with putting on a good show for the spectators who would pack into the gym for every game. Instead, he wanted to make sure that his players had a sound sense of rules and strategy, technique, instinct, and (most of all) teamwork. If those skills were in place, then the game unquestionably would be dynamic.

And so we drilled. And we drilled. And we drilled. We practiced everything until it was second nature to us. We didn't spend our time worrying about trick shots that might come in handy once a game; we spent the vast majority of our practice hours working on the most basic moves that carry the majority of the action in any basketball matchup—not just grasping them and moving on, but working until we had made them perfect. We ran three-on-twos and two-on-ones until we had mastered the basics of shooting, defending, and rebounding. There wasn't a secret formula; we just focused on becoming brilliant at the basics.

These practices were not simply sessions of rote repetition. Each one was a highly structured, precisely organized series of exercises carefully designed around certain essential elements. Coach Curtis was engaged in every step of the process. He walked around, shouting encouragement, or stopping to correct an incorrect stance or bad ball-handling habit. He made sure that practice was focused not on beating our next opponent, but on learning to play the game better. The rest would take care of itself.

These high school practices are almost certainly the source of my disinterest in poring over game reels from opponents. As Mr. Curtis had showed me, you win by becoming a better player of the game at large, not by adapting your technique to every new team you face. Your opponent will always be changing; it's a losing race. But if you master the game, you will have the skills and the knowledge you need to defeat whoever you are facing.

Thus it was from Mr. Curtis that I first became aware that a coach should ultimately be a teacher of the game. An English class can't teach you to write every phrase you might possibly need to compose in your professional life, but if the teacher gives you the skills you need to write a well-crafted document, you'll be able to call on those skills whenever you need to. The same is true for math. No math class will be able to present every equation you might ever have to figure, so you learn the technique. Once you master that, you'll be able to apply it to whatever scenario you might need to. Teaching sports is the same way: It is the principles you should study, not the specific situation.

I tried to apply this philosophy during my first few years as a high school teacher, as well, in a small town just over the state line, in Kentucky. I wanted to run a disciplined, organized classroom that prepared students by teaching them first the fundamentals and then the finer points. The same was true of my teams. I wanted to run practice the way Coach Curtis had done, so I organized our time around the basics and built from there.

It worked . . . kind of. I had some pretty good teams with very hard workers, but I felt that I wasn't quite capturing the example Mr. Curtis had set, and I wasn't sure what I was missing until a few years later when I was teaching in South Bend, Indiana.

I'd met the legendary Notre Dame football coach Frank Leahy at a local coaches' function a few months previously, and we'd just clicked. One day out of the blue he called and extended me an incredible opportunity: I was invited to watch his team practice. No one ever got to do this. No one. Not the media, not even local high school coaches. I still don't know why he made the offer, but I certainly wasn't going to turn it down.

I felt like I was crossing into a mysterious, hidden world as he walked me out to the practice fields. The players cycled from exercise to exercise without wasting time, without having to stop and ask for directions. Every player clearly understood what he was supposed to be working on, and every minute of practice had a designated goal. There was a plan; they stuck to it. There was no shuffling of notes, no haphazard transition from one drill to the next.

As I observed the scene in front of me, I suddenly experienced a tremendous sense of déjà vu. It was as if I was in the Martinsville High School gymnasium all over again, with Coach Curtis calling the shots. This was how he operated. This was how fundamental he really got: It wasn't just the players' skills that were sent back to basics; the coaches themselves focused on the fundamentals of time management and absolutely precise dictation of how the practice period would be divided.

I realized that I owed it to my students to make sure that every practice, every lesson, every moment in the classroom was planned down to the minute. This secret that Frank Leahy employed was the same that Glenn Curtis understood: The fundamentals matter for the players *and* the coach.

Once I had that realization, I recognized what was missing in my own teaching. I was taking too long in my explanations. Instead of repeatedly going through the instructions for how papers should be handed to the front of the classroom, I established a predictable pattern so that my students knew what to anticipate. That way, I didn't have to take the time to say, "When the time ends for the test, write your name clearly and pass the papers forward for me to collect." They already knew it and had done it. That was time saved for more important things.

The same was true on the court. My explanations were taking too long because I'd go on and on with the details and reminders and possible scenarios. I justified this approach because I believed it would help my players be better prepared for any eventuality the game might throw at them. But in reality, I didn't need to explain it every time. When Leahy called a drill, boom: The players were doing the drill. That was how things had been run under Coach Curtis. I started to adopt this technique into my own practices, where we had a routine for drilling the fundamentals, and the payoff in terms of how much we could accomplish in a short time was incredible.

Establishing the fundamentals keeps practices shorter because they can be more concentrated. Don't stop a group to explain to an individual what he's doing wrong. Pull him aside and instruct him. Don't ever hold a team past the established end of practice because they aren't performing up to standard. I never had a practice that went over two hours, and very few ever went more than even an hour and a half. We started on time and we stopped on time. And yet I think we got as much done as teams that spent far more time in the gym.

A large part of using time efficiently is creating a clear sense of expectations. You have made sure players know the order of the drills and what to focus on with each one. It's essential for challenging them; players tend to work harder throughout practice when they know what is expected of them, because they know what they are supposed to be doing and what the reason is behind it. In this manner, organization can be a way to create not just efficiency but also motivation.

It also builds teamwork, because it helps the players learn to think as one. They know what's coming, they know the routine, and that makes them feel a part of something bigger than themselves. The same is true in a classroom setting. The class feels a bond of experience because they all speak the same "language" of class routines and practices. Students speak up more when they feel comfortable in their class. Athletes play better when they feel connected to their team. An organized classroom, practice, or office can be one of the first steps toward developing this bond. A well-ordered atmosphere with clear goals can establish a positive dynamic that is hard to shake.

Glenn Curtis mentored me by setting this example in whatever he did. His organization didn't make him less personable or more removed; it just made me feel that my time was valued and my effort served a purpose. He never once sat his players down and explained to us, "This is how you run an effective practice." He simply did it, and we—and the rest of Martinsville—saw the results.

His demeanor during games had a similar mentoring effect on me. It's so easy to get caught up in what is commonly called "the passion of the moment." Energy can be infectious, and a little enthusiasm can quickly bring the bleachers to life. That is a wonderful thing—for the fans. But players and coaches need to keep their minds focused on the court, not the stands. That's exactly what Coach Curtis did. He managed to keep his composure, and in so doing, he taught me the important lesson that emotion should be kept off the court.

Especially in basketball, the direction of the game changes so quickly that it is essential for players to be able to keep a keen eye evaluating the game at all times. You learn the fundamentals as a team, but you have to operate on your own individual level of competence and at your own level of execution. If your emotions take over, you won't be able to do that because you are relying too much on the energy of other people rather than on confidence in your own skills.

For that reason, I learned from Coach Curtis that a coach should try to keep his players from being emotional in basketball. They need to play with spirit and with heart—that's a totally different subject. But if emotions such as anger, frustration, or overblown pride get in the way of control, the game is in trouble. Coach Curtis stressed to his players the importance of concentrating on the rest of the team and reading their signs, rather than getting swept away by the cheers or jeers that might be coming from the bleachers. He set the example by seeming to be completely unrattled by the noise around him. Don't get me wrong: He could get as excited as anyone; he was a joyous man who loved people and loved life. However, Coach Curtis rarely, if ever, seemed to lose his composure.

It's a little bit funny, I think, that some of the most important mentoring I received came in the form of not doing: Coach Curtis didn't react, didn't get shaken, didn't allow the circumstance to affect his self-possession. But mentoring doesn't always have to be about taking action. It also can be about showing self-control through *not* responding to a situation, by managing your own emotions. That was who Glenn Curtis was—a man who knew how to manage his time and his players and himself.

In that regard, he didn't have to do anything to be a mentor except to simply be himself. By teaching me how not to get caught up in certain things, he helped to shape one of the most recognized parts of my own coaching philosophy: staying in my seat and keeping my voice down, rather than pacing the sideline and screaming at players and referees. My father modeled it for me first; Coach Curtis showed me how to apply it to basketball.

This holds true for anyone who seeks to be a mentor or to be mentored themselves. Your not-doing can speak as loudly as your doing. You can teach with a quiet example just as well as you can teach with a dynamic one. Likewise, the best mentors are not always the most noticeable individuals but rather the ones who have shown the wisdom to react when action is called for and to avoid artificial excitement that can cloud a goal.

I have long said that I believe the best and most important coaching occurs in high school, because that is where the real teaching happens—where habits are established and where the fundamentals are emphasized in a different way than at higher levels. I think it can be more difficult to get a team to work together at the higher levels because there are more stand-out players on each squad, and those players tend to focus more on their statistics and their careers. I believe the old saying that the pros get you more money, and college gets you into the pros—but high school gets you into college.

It's funny, I guess, that Coach Curtis touched each one of those levels, starting as a high school coach before taking over as the athletic director and head basketball coach at Indiana State Teachers College. I can't think of a more fitting place for him to have taught the sport than at an institution dedicated to the creation of teachers. When I assumed the program from him in 1946, I found that he had done as much good work there as in Martinsville, establishing a culture of excellence at the school as a loved and respected coach for the fine example he set. He even worked in the pros for one year as the coach of the Detroit Falcons, a member of the Basketball Association of America, before retiring.

I haven't mentioned the fact that Coach Curtis never had a losing season in his entire career. Or that the Sycamores of Indiana State Teachers College won the Midwest Invitational Tournament in 1946. Or that he coached eighteen years at Martinsville and won fifteen sectionals, twelve regionals, and three state titles. Or that his career winning percentage was 78. I haven't mentioned any of that because that's not what he was about.

His legacy was not the statistics he left, though they are impressive, but the style of coaching he brought to the game. His greatest impact was not on the national stage, but at Martinsville High School, where in 1959, the legendary gym was renamed the Glenn M. Curtis Memorial Gymnasium in his honor. His was a life that taught by example, where coaching was teaching and where winning was incidental—though it was an incident that came about with incredible frequency!

Coach Curtis will always have a place in my memory as an even-keeled, even-tempered, and even-minded man. The lessons he taught me were some of the most fundamental of my own professional and personal life. He didn't have to discipline me, the way my father did; or humble me, as Earl Warriner did. Those earlier mentors laid the groundwork so I would be ready for and receptive to the lessons I needed to learn later in life. Glenn Curtis taught me how to teach.

In many ways, he was the real secret of my success.

CHAPTER 5

. . . .

Piggy Lambert

IN RETROSPECT, IT SEEMS IRONIC that a rather small man (he stood only five feet six inches tall) would revolutionize the sport of basketball by inventing innovative ways to use "big man" players. But Ward "Piggy" Lambert never seemed to see limitations—only possibilities.

With him, I gained one of the most important mentors of my career. From Coach Lambert, I learned the philosophies that were to become my trademark both on and off the court: conditioning, skill, and team spirit. He demonstrated the importance of unity and cohesion for making a team, and this was a lesson I never forgot. He modeled the importance of decisive action and taking risks, but he also cautioned us not to be reckless. He showed us responsibility, compassion, and (perhaps above all else) how to bring your personal principles into your career.

His voice, his ideas, and his influence still loom large in my memory. Coach Lambert not only helped to sculpt my game; he also recognized in me the need I felt for direction and advice as a young man away from home facing important decisions. His example gave me both the immediate counsel I craved and the confidence to trust my own instincts. As a mentor, he was a giant.

RECRUITING FOR COLLEGE athletics was a completely different world in the 1920s and 1930s. If you were a good player graduating from high school, a few head coaches from schools in your geographical region might contact you; if they were really interested, they would come out to your house and visit with your family, and then you would make a decision. Campus visits, which are now an essential element of recruitment, simply weren't part of the process; neither were athletic scholarships. Thus my decision to attend Purdue was based almost entirely on my impression of Coach Lambert.

I was All-State my senior year of high school, which granted me a little more notoriety than I might otherwise have gotten as a small-town player. As a result, I'd been recruited by Notre Dame and Indiana University, as well as by Purdue, and each school was tempting for its own reasons.

Notre Dame, of course, was a big name, then in the middle of its first real athletic heyday. Indiana, on the other hand, was only seventeen miles from home, so I would have been much closer to my high school sweetheart, Nellie, who was a year younger than I and hadn't yet graduated. The head coaches at all three schools seemed like very good men from whom I could have learned a great deal, but there was just something about Piggy Lambert that stood out to me and made me feel that he was the man I wanted to play for. Maybe it was that we shared a love for baseball—he'd even played semiprofessionally and earned his nickname for "gobbling up" every ball that came his way on the field. Maybe it was because he stressed academics before athletics. But I think it was his principles.

Living with my father had shown me the importance of

living by your convictions, and when I saw that same trait re-
flected in a prospective coach, I knew the match was right. The
way he spoke with my family and with me made it clear he
wasn't concerned with making me a star athlete; he wanted to
help make me a man. That was the first lesson I ever learned
from Coach Lambert: A coach's primary function should be not
to make better players, but to make better people.

I STARTED AT Purdue as a civil engineering major. Ever since I
was a child, I had been fascinated with the idea of building, and
the career excited me as a way to create important things such
as tall bridges and wide highways—the kinds of things that
seem exotic and glamorous to rural farm boys from Indiana.

But I didn't know that civil engineering students had to attend a camp over the summer for further study. This wasn't an
option for me. I was always working at that time, even during
the school year in between practices and classes, trying to earn
enough money to cover my bills. Coach Lambert respected that
and allowed me to keep it up because I never allowed it to in-
terfere with my performance on the court. But leisure time during the summer was a luxury I simply didn't have; I had to work
during those months to earn my money for the next semester.
So at the end of my freshman year, I realized I would have to
drop civil engineering and take up another major. I'd had a wonderful literature professor named Dr. Creek, whose class made
me realize my love for fine writing in a whole new way—so I decided to become an English major. And the moment I did so, I
just knew I would be a teacher.

All that summer between my freshman and sophomore years
I worked for the state highway department, learning more
about building roads and civil construction than I would ever
have learned in a camp. But it didn't matter; by that time, my

childhood love of literature and poetry had been reawakened; I was dead set on the idea of being a teacher, and Coach Lambert seemed to know it. I think I was happier in practice and more relaxed on the court. I had found my calling, and it was simultaneously exciting and comforting.

I started watching Coach Lambert in a different way, trying not only to learn from him as a player, but also to study how he coached and what made him effective as the leader of a team. These were all things I knew would be important to me when I started teaching at a high school and would hopefully be able to take over a team of my own.

We enjoyed a great deal of success my first two years on the team. Charles "Stretch" Murphy, who at six-six was one of the first real "big men" of the game, scored 143 points to set the Big Ten scoring record in 1929, and we went 10–0 to win the Big Ten title in 1930. I loved being a part of that team, and the Purdue fans loved to watch us play.

One day, toward the end of my sophomore year, Coach Lambert called me into his office to let me know that a certain prominent doctor in town wanted to sponsor me, covering my expenses so I wouldn't have to work. The stringent rules about collegiate athletes receiving gifts didn't really exist then, so the offer was perfectly legal. Coach Lambert laid out the doctor's proposal before me and asked what I thought about it.

"What does he want me to do to pay him back?"

"Nothing," Coach said. "He just likes you and wants to help you out."

He knew what it would mean to me if I didn't have to work: No more waiting tables at fraternity houses for fifty dollars a month to cover the tuition, room and board, and other expenses. I did have an academic scholarship, but it didn't cover everything. I could even go back to the civil engineering program if I wanted to.

After thinking it over for a few days, I returned to Coach's office. "I've got along all right thus far," I told him. "So I guess I'm going to turn it down."

I'll never forget how Coach Lambert responded to that: He smiled and said, "I knew you'd say that." I think he understood how important my pride was, and how I had been raised to never be beholden to anyone else. By laying out the terms of the agreement before me, he allowed me to see what was out there for me, but to also make the decision on my own. It was exactly the kind of guidance and trust I needed.

But Coach Lambert would not allow me to be too hard on myself, either. "You do need some clothes badly," he pointed out. "You almost froze when we went up to Minnesota last year, and your shoes aren't good. Go to the department store and get yourself some new ones. It's already set up for you."

Noticing the look of confusion on my face, he laughed. "It's not a gift. You're entitled to two tickets for each game next year, right? Well, he'll be getting those instead. It's a trade, and you owe him nothing. And don't worry," he added. "If Nellie or your parents want to come up for a game, we'll make sure they get in."

I left that day feeling I had just experienced an incredible lesson in coach-player interaction. Coach Lambert had shown that he believed me mature enough to make the right decision, rather than the easy one. At the same time, he also had recognized a physical need and found a way to make sure I was taken care of. He let me be an adult but also understood that I was still young. Confidence and compassion—he knew I needed both.

THAT INCIDENT ALSO taught me another important lesson on interacting with players. My coach had taken the time to really get to know me, to know how I would respond, and to pay attention to what I needed. Coach Lambert always let us know that he genuinely cared for us. He would ask how parents were doing and if there were any health concerns; he knew our girlfriends and our siblings by name.

I remain convinced to this day that compassion like that—sincerely caring for your players and maintaining an active interest in their lives, concerns, and motivations—is one of the most important qualities a coach can have.

Coach Lambert never neglected to talk to us about our personal lives. He wouldn't probe if a topic was clearly sensitive, but he was attentive to anything that might be distracting us from fully concentrating on a game. If it was trouble in a class or trouble in a relationship, he just seemed to know what to ask. And feeling that the coach cared enough about us to find out and wanted to check with us to make sure everything was all right meant that we could relax a bit, knowing that there was someone on our side. I know he did it because he cared about us, first and foremost; but I think he got better performance out of us as an added benefit of giving us a chance to vent.

AND PERFORMANCE WAS, after all, something that Coach Lambert stressed more than any other coach I'd ever had. His players quickly learned that basketball was not just about skills and technique but also about the fundamentals of athletic ability. We conditioned more than any other team we faced.

We ran as part of each practice to build up stamina, giving us a key advantage in the second half of games. "It won't pay off in the beginning," he'd tell us. "But before the end of each half and especially in the second half of play, you'll feel the difference if you're conditioned." Sensing that we didn't quite believe that Indiana University coach Everett Dean's emphasis on things other than physical training would really give us that much of an advantage, he added, "When we play Indiana University, we'll beat them because Coach Dean is too kind and he doesn't work his players hard enough. We'll get to them at the end of each half." Would you know it—he was absolutely right!

Coach Lambert really believed in building athletes from the ground up, a philosophy I carried with me to my own coaching. Besides conditioning, we also worked on the fundamentals with quickness drills in movement and passing and shooting; quickness in moving with the ball, quickness in moving without the ball; quickness on defense and quickness on offense. Quickness was stressed in everything. The team that had its fundamentals down to perfection could afford to move with more speed, which meant more chances at the basket. It may sound simple, but it sure worked.

Team spirit was his other big focus. If you didn't play in a way that lifted the team, you would be sitting on the bench, no matter who you were. I'm proud to say I never had to sit out for that reason, but I think that stemmed in large part from the fact that I knew he wasn't bluffing. More than once I saw a top player get pulled from a game and placed on the bench until he cooled off and remembered he was part of a team. This really made an impression on me.

As I was consciously making an effort to absorb strong coaching techniques in anticipation of my own career, I was subconsciously filing away the elements that years later would come together to form my Pyramid of Success—the outline of characteristics and practices I devised to illustrate how a person can achieve personal success in his or her own life. Just as I had while watching my father and my previous coaches, I was making a note of the traits that seemed to be the most important, and the most universal, in successful individuals. Conditioning, skill, quickness, execution, and team play—the philosophies I learned from watching Coach Lambert interact with us—became the basis of my pyramid.

Even though he was equally willing to bench the star and the backup if they weren't working as team players, Coach Lambert showed me the importance of tailoring one's coaching style to each individual athlete. There were some players who responded better to short, frank instructions ("Stop flicking your wrist to peck the ball at the net!") and others who responded to a gentler tone ("Next time, I want you to try to roll the ball off your fingertips and see if that doesn't help you make the shot better."). Because he had taken the time to really get to know us, he understood what manner of correction would yield the best results from each player.

He also adapted his game technique to the talent he had on his bench. Every coach has a system that he or she prefers to use. For Coach Lambert, it was the fast break, which he developed and popularized. But if he found he had a player who did better with a different strategy, he would adjust the game plan accordingly.

This would be an essential part of my own coaching. For thirty-four of my forty years of coaching, I used a high post offense. Using that system, I learned how to run reverses better and how to run screens and rolls better. But for the other six years I used a high-low post because, frankly, it better fit the talents of my players at the time. If a player's outside jumps were off or unreliable, I'd make a note to keep working on that, but would change the role of the plays for that upcoming game until we could address the issue in practice. You have to be willing to adjust.

Even when we stuck with one strategy, we made sure it was flexible. In the high post offense, when we had stronger forwards, we would tend to give the forwards more shots. If the guards were better, we'd shift it to them. Maybe we'd do a combination. Treating people equally does not mean coaching them the same. If you don't adjust to the personnel you have, you're losing something, no matter how good they are. You have to adapt your plans to the players you have so their unique talents can contribute to the team.

And there is another element to this equation: You've got to be realistic about your expectations—not only on the court, but also in life. A few years after I graduated from college, I received a phone call from Coach Lambert regarding my youngest brother, Billy. Danny, the third in line after Maurice and me, had gone off to New Mexico Teachers College, even though Maurice and I had wanted him to stay closer to home; but Billy had followed in my footsteps and chosen Purdue. He also was on the basketball team, playing for Coach Lambert—a decision that made me incredibly proud. But one day, during Billy's sophomore year, I got that phone call from Coach. "Billy's not happy," he told me. "He knows he's not going to play much and he wants to drop basketball, but he's afraid that will hurt you. Could you talk to him?"

I felt terrible. It had *never* been my intention for Billy to play just out of guilt. I'd love him every bit as much if he didn't play as if he did—but I'd been so excited about the idea of having a brother play for the same team and the same coach I loved so well that I hadn't stopped to consider if it was really the best thing for Billy.

At Coach Lambert's request, I gave Billy a call, and he did end up deciding to drop basketball. I'll admit that it hurt me a little to see him leave it behind, since he was a pretty good player. But I had to accept that Billy's decision had to be his own, and I couldn't let it be about what I wanted for him. While all of my brothers were talented athletes, Maurice and I were probably a little bit better than the younger two, and I'm sure it was tough for Danny and Billy to always feel like they were in our shadows.

I've always been grateful that Coach Lambert recognized that my brother was struggling and needed someone to talk to—and, more, that *I* needed to let Billy lead his own life, whether or not it corresponded with what I wanted for him.

But that was just Coach Lambert's way—he perceived enough to adapt, he cared enough to understand, and he was still managing to mentor me, even though I was both miles away and years past our time together at Purdue.

OF COURSE, I was not the only person to benefit from having Coach Lambert as a mentor. His 1932 book *Practical Basketball*, one of the earliest and best of the "how-to" manuals, was carried in suit jackets and gym bags all across the country, by coaches and players at every level of the game. (I'm sure it's easy to understand why my first book on fundamentals and style of team play was titled *Practical Modern Basketball*.)

Nineteen thirty-two—my senior season—also was the year when the Purdue Boilermakers were voted the National Champions (NCAA tournament play didn't begin until 1939). It was an amazing season for us, and a wonderful time for the rest of the basketball world to celebrate the innovative techniques and philosophies of Piggy Lambert.

I laugh, now, that we had no idea just how far ahead of his time Coach Lambert really was. When Nike launched their "Just Do It" slogan in 1988, I thought, "That's what Coach Lambert was saying all along!"

"The doer makes mistakes," he would say. "Mistakes come from doing, but so does success." He stressed the importance of acting rather than overanalyzing. That's why fundamentals were so key for him. If your body was already conditioned to have everything else positioned as it should be, you could trust your instincts in a high-pressure game situation.

I think there is a lesson there for everyone, on or off the court: If something needs to be done, do it. If there is something you think might be beneficial for those around you, be the one to act; don't wait for someone else to do it. Take action and take initiative. It can be passing the ball, or it can be striking up a conversation with a lonely neighbor—whatever the situation, we all should have the fundamentals in line so we can seize the moment and act.

And *never* let your fear of failure prevent you from going forward. One of my favorite lessons from Coach Lambert is that the team that makes more mistakes is probably the team that wins the game. There are risks and there will be mistakes, but if you've conditioned for them, the victories will outweigh the losses. I firmly believe that this is true for just about any situation in athletics or in life; if your principles are solid, you can approach any opportunity with confidence.

I've told a particular story about Coach Lambert's influence in my life with regard to stressing the importance of teamwork. But when I consider his importance as a mentor, I have begun to see that the story takes on additional significance.

When I was coaching the Sycamores of Indiana State Teachers College in the 1940s, my team was invited to play in the National Association of Intercollegiate Basketball (NAIB) tournament—a real honor and a chance for my small school to be in the national spotlight. There was one condition, however: All players had to be white. I declined the invitation, citing the presence of Clarence Walker, an African American student who was part of the Sycamore team. A team is a team, I told the NAIB, and rules must reflect that. To leave one member behind—especially one who was hardworking both on the court and in the classroom—because of a discriminatory policy would go against not only my conscience, but also everything I had emphasized to my players about the importance of sticking together.

When the Sycamores were invited to the tournament again the following year, Clarence Walker was allowed to take the court, too. The influence of Piggy Lambert's lessons didn't just strengthen a team; it also helped to push college athletics one step forward. It was certainly a risk—I might have been ostracized and my school disinvited from any future tournaments. But I stood by my principles because I knew I was right. My fundamentals were in line, so I could act with confidence. That confidence was something I had gained from my own college coach a decade before, and that I hoped my students were now gaining from me.

THE FLIP SIDE of being a doer is, of course, making sure that you are not reckless. Coach Lambert stressed that, too. His philosophy was about acting not on impulse, but on strong principles.

There's a great illustration of this: While I was still an undergraduate, I was approached by scouts for both the Cubs and the Reds about playing minor-league baseball with their organizations. It was a tempting offer that dangled a solid salary and certain adventure in front of me, and I was sure Coach Lambert would be as excited about it as I was. But when I went to talk to him about it, his reaction was cooler than I'd anticipated. He responded with a question: "Did you come here for an education?"

"Yes, sir."

"And what is the goal of that education?"

"To become a teacher, sir."

"And how will this help you toward reaching that goal?"

He had me there. Coach Lambert had been on the minor-league baseball circuit himself, so he knew very well what would be facing me there. He knew where I stood in my relationship with Nellie and what I owed my family for helping me through school, and he knew where I would have a future and where I would have only a couple of years of fun. He let me make my own decision, but just as in the scenario with the generous doctor, he knew which way I'd choose.

What it comes down to, I believe, is that mentoring often involves telling people what they need to hear, rather than what they want to hear. When you are able to be humbly honest with someone about a situation with which you have personal experience—even if you risk angering or hurting that person— you are offering the most valuable gift of all. That's what mentors do: They offer up their own experiences for the benefit of others. It's recognizing that someone or something has come along and set you right or shown you a reality, and you are then paying the favor forward. It's admitting that you needed instruction at one point, too. That can be humbling, but the best leaders are usually humble leaders because they gain loyalty through respect rather than bravado. Offer whatever you can that is worthy of respect. Mentoring isn't about celebrating your own insight but about sharing wisdom. When you pass on the lessons of your life with someone else, it's not you who are teaching—it's your experience.

That's what Ward "Piggy" Lambert showed me that day in his office, and every day we interacted. It's always about what is best for the team. It's always about focusing not on the mistakes but on the lessons learned from them. Mentoring is never about the mentor; it's always about the mentee.

In *Practical Basketball*, Lambert wrote that the coach has a responsibility to "be a teacher of good habits." If ever there was a coach who lived by those words, it was the man who penned them.

CHAPTER 6

Mother Teresa

Ultimately, as we watch those around us who become our mentors, we will begin to notice certain behaviors, practices, or philosophies that are universal. There are certain things that all great leaders seem to share, though they may manifest themselves differently depending on the life and circumstances of each individual.

We can all benefit from studying the lives of great men and women. Their courage, vision, and actions can serve to mentor us in a different kind of way—we can seek them out. A person cannot always choose who will surround him or her in life. We always can choose what biographies to pull from a shelf, or what studies to seek in the library. Sometimes we select the mentor for the lessons we want to learn. And the mentor doesn't have to be someone who is physically present in your life. It isn't necessary to have ever actually met an individual to have been mentored by him or her.

What, after all, is the point of publishing works on the lives of historical figures if not to offer the readers something to learn from them? But the education gained does

not have to be simply an academic one; it also can be an
education of character. I discovered that to be true as I
studied the lives of two tremendous figures, one religious
and one political—and both mentors to me.

THERE IS, PERHAPS, NO GREATER illustration of love, faith, and devotion in the modern world than that of a tiny, wrinkled figure who lived among lepers and pariahs in the slums of Calcutta. I'm referring, of course, to Mother Teresa.

Her life is a shining example of the greatness of humility, as she has inspired thousands of others toward works of service; even through the dark periods of her life, when nothing seemed to shine, her humanity has been a beacon to thousands who feel a similar struggle of doubt, pain, and hopelessness.

Throughout my life and in my own journey of faith, I have found that the example of Mother Teresa is always there before me, uplifting me and spurring me on, even as I would try to encourage my players to hold fast to their beliefs. Some of those beliefs are supreme, such as a belief in God. Others are more mundane, such as a belief that we all have a responsibility to care for those around us—something no less profound. All those beliefs are intertwined, and it is with these lessons that the tiny nun from Calcutta became my mentor.

I CAN'T SAY exactly when I found myself growing interested in Mother Teresa. In fact, I'm not even sure when I became aware of her work apart from her tremendous character. The same is true, I suppose, for many of the other tremendous figures I find fascinating, such as Mahatma Gandhi and Helen Keller—it's impossible to know exactly when I first learned of their stories.

I just realized in looking back that somewhere along the way they made an impression that stayed with me.

With Mother Teresa, I suddenly became aware that I was contemplating her example a great deal and eagerly searching out any information I could find about her. Every interview with her that I read, every quotation she made to the press seemed to reach out and grab me with the conviction of "Yes! This is what I feel but have not been able to give shape in words." I felt a burning need to learn more about her.

The first quote from Mother Teresa that really stayed with me was "Unless a life is lived for others, it is not worthwhile." The more I thought about this statement, the more its simple truth became apparent: Each of us has a responsibility to lead our life with a focus beyond ourselves. We cannot all start orphanages or establish clinics, of course, but every one of us can serve others, whether by meeting their physical needs or their emotional ones. An insulated life that never reaches out is something of a waste—life should be a complex network of relationships and encounters that all serve to grow an individual and others.

Mentoring can happen whenever there is a lesson to be shared, even if the lesson is something as basic as showing love. And love itself comes in a variety of forms. It can take the shape of patience, or it can take the shape of respect—two traits essential for teachers and students alike. Love can take the shape of a genuine inquiry of "How are you doing?" This is a question we tend to toss out as a kind of greeting without expecting an honest answer in return. But just by letting people know that you truly do care how they are feeling, you are showing them love and reminding them that they are not alone. Mother Teresa did this for the poor in the Indian slums—people no one else in the world seemed to care about at all. By showing love to the unloved, she also showed millions of people how profound an impact even the simplest action of kindness can have, and the dignity it can grant the suffering.

Why did the world find her to be such a fascinating figure? Why did we read articles about her and watch documentaries on her work? Surely it was not because the conditions of poverty in developing nations is a pleasant subject. No, I think Mother Teresa became such a dynamic figure because she did what anyone could have done but what no one else would do. She reminded us of our own ability to care and the impact of even the most simple act. "If you can't feed a hundred people," she often remarked, "then feed just one."

We are all called to give back. Since there is nothing we can take with us from this life, we should try to leave behind as much as possible—it's a basic and well-known truth. Those of us who have been blessed with worldly success have an even greater responsibility to make an impact with our time, talents, and resources; as we are reminded in the Gospels, "From him to whom much is given, much is required."

I believe that much is expected of me. I enjoyed tremendous success during my coaching career, all stemming from my ability to teach from the heart. And yet, one of the best things about my retirement is that it has allowed me to devote more time to the causes that mean the most to me. I retired from coaching, but not from teaching. Even now, I seek out opportunities that will allow me a chance to share the blessings God has been good enough to grant me through a long and eventful life.

While I was coaching, I was surrounded by some of the most gifted and exceptional young men in the country— outstanding examples of student athletes, sound in body and mind and rich in discipline. And I taught them everything I was able. But now I find that there are other athletes who need me just as much. They are very different from the players I coached at UCLA in almost every way imaginable, but they deserve the same careful teaching. The Special Olympics is an organization with which I love to work not only because it promotes athletics and sportsmanship—ideas I greatly valued in my own coaching—but also because it reaches out to individuals with special needs and lets them know that they are loved, valued, and important. It gives them dignity, and it reminds everyone involved of the beautiful place that patience and gentleness should have in our lives. I can think of little else more worthwhile than that.

I also find myself drawn to other organizations such as Ronald McDonald House and various children's hospitals. We are fortunate enough not to have people suffering from leprosy on the streets in America, but we do have countless children suffering from cancer, in need of organ transplants, or facing any number of other devastating diseases.

Any gesture of love, any effort made on behalf of their health or the comfort of their family while they endure the hospitalization is in some sense as significant as the work of Mother Teresa's Missionaries of Charity. We all share the same goal, after all, whether we are serving in the dirty streets of Calcutta or the sterile hallways of a pediatric ward, or holding a stopwatch by a hot track where special individuals are assembled to race—we want to offer a word of kindness and a hand of love to people who have no means to repay us.

That is the most central lesson I can take from Mother Teresa's life of service: You should never expect a reward in return. The gift is reward enough for the giver. I remember, in fact, making a resolution after reading another story about Mother Teresa's work that I would strive to do one kind thing each day for someone who could never return the favor. And it is a challenge I have issued to many others since then.

If we agree with Mother Teresa that a life not lived for others is not worthwhile, then a day lacking just one simple deed for others is certainly not a complete day. One must assemble a life one day, and one deed, at a time.

MOTHER TERESA PRESENTED a tremendous example in how she lived her own beliefs. But there is another, very different way that she offered me important life lessons: by respecting the beliefs of others. It can be difficult, as a coach, to handle the various religions of my players with equal sensitivity and understanding. I am simply not familiar enough with the practices and rituals of other faiths to make absolutely certain I do not inadvertently say or do something that disrespects the religious practices of a player and thus cause him to stumble in his beliefs, such as scheduling a practice during a holy day. I never wanted my players to feel as if they had to choose between basketball and their religious conscience.

Mother Teresa opened the Home for the Dying in Calcutta as a place where the poor of any religion could come to live their final days in dignity and pass into the next life in comfort. They were offered medical care and the final rituals of their own faith. Roman Catholics would receive Last Rites; Hindus would be given water from their sacred river, the Ganges; and Muslims would be read to from the Koran.

She found that the individuals who came to her in this difficult period in their life needed to be treated where they were, both physically and spiritually; it was her job not to steer their beliefs but simply to offer them peace. This philosophy was so beautiful to me, and I could empathize deeply with it, on a much less dire level, of course. Oftentimes, probably because of the period of life in which my players came to me, I found many young men at a crossroads in their religious beliefs.

I always tried to be sensitive to this, as I realize it is something many parents worry about, too. If I knew a family to be particularly religious, I would try to arrange for one of my assistant coaches with a similar religious background to do the recruiting visits. My assistant coaches were usually men of faith themselves, and I felt that it was important for parents to see that if, say, the family was Catholic, their son would have a strong Catholic figure as part of the team. It wasn't a recruiting gimmick; it was a sensitivity to the valid and important concerns that surround religion.

There was one evening I will always remember, because it was one of the most moving experiences of my years as a coach. We had played at Ohio State on a Saturday and had to get to Notre Dame the next day for another game. The weather was bad as we piled onto the bus, ready to drive through the night into Sunday morning. We all had hot chocolate and sandwiches—hardly spectacular dining, but as we drove off toward South Bend, I watched as all of our religions started to be expressed as individuals began their personal worship. There were Protestants and Catholics and Mormons and Jews, and even one young man (Lewis Alcindor, better known as Kareem Abdul-Jabbar) who would convert to Islam just a few years later. As each player began his own private devotions, so did the others, until the bus was filled with the quiet sound of a dozen different voices, each reaching up to God in his own way. It was awe-inspiring and humbling.

After the devotions drew to a close, the players began to ask each other about their various practices, until intense and interested conversations developed about beliefs and rituals. I was impressed at how much some players, like Lewis, knew about Mormonism and other faiths. Other players had very little knowledge but a great deal of curiosity.

I kept silent, just listening to them talk and marveling at the wonderful unity I think we all felt. Eventually they asked me to join the conversations, which I did. But I was careful not to add too much, or to change the nature of the conversations in any way. The simple curiosity and the respectful, reverential tone that seemed to surround them were so moving to experience, and so delicate in their nature, that I preferred to let them run their own course than to try to force them to become anything else.

I have imagined since then that Mother Teresa must have had a similar image in mind when she established her Home for the Dying—each person practicing the devotions of his or her faith on the stormy road from one place to the next destination.

Her example has been an important one for me in that regard. She showed me that I am not being untrue to my own religion if I do not actively seek to convert those around me to my own beliefs. It was never my desire to talk my players into or out of any kind of faith. I was called upon, instead, to offer guidance to help them figure it out on their own.

Young adulthood is a challenge for many people. It is a period of coming into your own and deciding who you really are and who you are going to be, free of the dictates of your parents. College affords a different kind of freedom and exposure to new ideas, during which many students choose to explore a different denomination or a different faith or even to stop practicing religion at all. As a result, I had quite a few players over the years come to me with religious struggles and ask for advice. The last thing I wanted to do was to steer them wrong.

One particular player, Keith Wilkes, stands out to me. You could not find a finer individual than Keith—an outstanding student, an All-American player, a polite and respectful young man. He came to talk to me one day because he was thinking about changing his religion, and he wanted my advice. This was a particularly sensitive topic for him, I think, because his father was a minister.

I asked Keith what he believed, how his views were chang-ing, and what he thought might have caused this new perspec-tive. We talked for quite a while. Finally I just said to him, "You have to have a reason for believing what you do. You need to fig-ure out what that reason is and what's wrong at the present, and see if you can reach a resolution." I also talked to his father, not betraying Keith's confidence, but just to make him aware that his son might be seeking his guidance.

I emerged from the conversation with a new perspective on how to discuss religion with my players. I would never initiate the conversation, but if they approached me for advice—and many did—I would tell them, "Have something to believe in; have a reason to believe in it, but stay open-minded." I felt that this last piece of advice was especially important. It wouldn't re-quire great change of everyone; for some people, it might mean just being willing to show respect for and sensitivity to others. For some players, though, it might mean that they needed to seek out a faith that was their own and not inherited from their parents. And for still others, it might mean that though they were going through a religious transition and seeking to get rid of old ideas, they might eventually find that those truths are the very ones to which they wanted to return, and they needed to be open to that.

As long as my players were practicing a faith or seeking one, I was content. Every faith, after all, has some manifestation of the Golden Rule; and if there was one thing I wanted my players to practice both on and off the court, it was to treat others in the same manner that they themselves would like to be treated.

It was not my place to direct my players to take one route or another with their faith. A coerced faith is not a genuine one. A mentor must always guide, never push. It was my job to listen to them, offer my perspective, and encourage them to pursue the ideals they believed to be true.

The example put into place in the slums of Calcutta provided me with the greatest possible example of how to serve diverse needs in a manner that was true to my own, and that
allowed my players to be true to theirs.

BUT IT IS not only Mother Teresa's pious moments that have
given me comfort. A few years ago, her personal diary was
published, and its pages contained striking moments of doubt
when she felt that God had deserted her and periods of questioning when she asked Him if He even existed at all. Many
people were upset, feeling that the publication of the document was just a stunt by her critics to discredit her work
and besmirch her name. When these writings were released,
however—in a 2007 book, *Mother Teresa: Come Be My Light*—I
remember hearing that people found tremendous comfort in
her words, because they showed how a person can persevere
through low times and, by continuing her acts of kindness, re-
discover the face of God in a new and more meaningful way.
The answer during times of doubt is not to walk away from service to others, but to seek it out even more than before.

I believe that the raw, naked honesty of that diary mentored
the world every bit as much as did her example of charity. It is
important for us to see that our mentors are human and therefore fallible; it makes our own shortcomings more tenable.

It can be upsetting when, as children, we first discover that
our parents are not perfect. It can shake our worldview when
we learn that a hero we idolized was not quite as perfect as we
thought. But it can strengthen us, too. As I have already discussed, an important part of being mentored is learning from
the mistakes of others. Hand in hand with that, though, comes
the knowledge we gain by watching how others work to rise
above their shortcomings. If we are surrounded by flawless

individuals, it can make our own mistakes seem magnified. And if a problem appears overlarge, it becomes more intimidating to attempt to overcome it.

There are several ways in which I have found comfort in the example of Mother Teresa. The first is in my initial acceptance of faith. My religious beliefs are an integral part of my life, coaching, and teaching. But it would be wrong to imagine that this was always true. We went to church every Sunday when I was a boy, and my parents were very devout people, reading to us from the Bible and stressing the model of Christ in their conduct. I followed their example.

I believed in God and Jesus, of course, but I didn't really understand the humble submission required of Christians until later in my life. There was no revelation where everything changed—no Damascus road moment when things suddenly became clear for me. It was more of a belief that grew with me until it was complete. Even now I would be hard pressed to answer exactly when I fully accepted Christ. I just trust He realizes that I did eventually.

Sometimes, when I considered the amazing examples of faith in my life, such as my parents and my wife, I wondered what was wrong with me. Why was my belief less visible or passionate than theirs, even if I knew it was as real and as deeply held? Learning of Mother Teresa's personal religious struggles felt like a weight being lifted from my soul. Faith takes a different shape in each of us, and though I may have a quieter belief, that makes it no less authentic and no less important. It just means that God works within me in a different way.

Many people have questioned whether Mother Teresa would have wanted her private writings to be broadcast to the world in such a way, and I think it is very likely that she would not have been pleased at all—unless she could have seen the effects they had. Surely a woman who lived to help others would have been pleased to witness the assistance that her words have offered to so many.

This, too, is a lesson in mentoring. Even in the midst of our own struggles, we can offer encouragement. Even during our personal low periods, we can continue to try to be a mentor to those around us. If we are honest about what we are facing, we can offer hope to others that they are not alone.

It is hard to admit, but I struggled tremendously with my religious beliefs after Nellie died. It was difficult to grasp how a benevolent God could have allowed her to suffer so much at the end, or how He could expect me to go on living without her. I had often found myself (and sometimes still find myself) questioning God when some kind of unspeakable tragedy occurs—an earthquake striking an impoverished area in Asia, or a hurricane destroying an orphanage in Central America. How can God allow such things? The tragedy does not even have to be on such a large scale. I wrestle with the idea of how a loving God could let a teenager lose a limb in a car accident, or a child suffer from leukemia. The question of pain has always weighed heavily on my soul.

But losing Nellie was the worst for me, because it wasn't just that she was taken from me, it was that I had to watch her suffer first. I cried out to God again and again, asking how He could permit her to endure so much pain. What good could possibly come from that? How was it fair that a woman who had dedicated her life so fully to Him should have to meet such a difficult end? And, of course, what would I ever do without her in my life when He did finally take her home?

I never did receive direct answers to those questions. Sometimes they still beleaguer me. I feel that perhaps God means for me not to share my perfectly contented worldview, but rather to admit to my struggle so that others, too, can know that they are not alone with such questions. This is why the Book of Job is contained within the Bible, so we can all learn from a righteous man who suffered the loss of his family, belongings, and health—and, though in his struggles he questioned God, never cursed Him.

Perhaps we can view Mother Teresa as a modern-day version of that same story. The example of her good works and righteousness would be lesson enough for us, but we get a more complete picture of her life with the story of her suffering. Her good works can inspire us, but her struggles can teach us.

As GREAT A mentor as Mother Teresa was and is, we know about her because the media were there to help spread the word. I do not doubt that there are many other people as dedicated to service and love as she was, working all over the globe. That's true in any walk of life; I don't question that I'll never hear of some of the finest teachers and coaches in this country, simply because there isn't anyone stepping up to tell their story.

This presents a challenge and an opportunity for us all to look around and consider what wonderful people we have surrounding us, and what incredible mentoring opportunities they have to offer. There are tremendous lessons to learn from the great people of the world, but there are just as many to be learned from the quiet people around us.

"We shall never know all the good that a simple smile can do," Mother Teresa once said. A smile may seem like an inconsequential thing, but it is a starting place, a first step. She reminded me of this every time I saw her picking up a child or holding a spoon for an invalid. We are all called to do more, but we must begin somewhere. Despite the tremendous global scope of her work and mission, it all started with something small: a desire to serve. So must we all make that first commitment toward action, toward encouragement, toward love. It may be something as simple as a smile, but even a smile is something. And with that one tiny gesture of a smile, you, too, are teaching the lesson of joy—and in her own words, "Joy is a net of love by which you catch souls."

Mother Teresa also famously remarked, "You can do no great things, only small things with great love." That is, after all, the lesson of mentoring. It is the small acts of teaching, infused with genuine care, that touch a life, which in turn touches another. And in this way, through the small acts, the simple gestures, the humble service, the learning and the mentoring, we each can have an impact far greater than any of us could imagine.

CHAPTER 7

Abraham Lincoln

W HEN YOU PICTURE PRESIDENT Lincoln, chances are good that the iconic image of a solemn man with a craggy, lined face comes to mind. We rarely think of Lincoln as a laughing or lively man, or even a particularly happy one—and he probably wasn't. But he wasn't humorless; in the more than sixteen thousand books about his life, history has recorded a number of his clever and witty remarks. However, he was consumed with the political whirlwind of the mid-1800s, and it is the deep sense of responsibility and the weight of moral agony that we see etched in Lincoln's face.

But in this same face, we also see insight and wisdom, and in his life we see character and integrity. Over the course of my career, I have had the opportunity to meet several presidents; through books, I have had the privilege of being mentored by one. The legacy of the sixteenth president still reverberates throughout twenty-first-century America, and the legacy of Lincoln, a tenacious, emotional, and humble man, echoes in my life every day.

LINCOLN, I'VE READ, was interested in Thomas Jefferson and sought out many of the same books that Jefferson had in his personal library to learn more about how he thought and how he viewed the world. Their political lives never overlapped, even though their professions took a similar route. And yet Lincoln recognized the importance of a strong example, so he sought it out. My father did the same with Lincoln. He studied Lincoln's life and writings and espoused many of his great traits. Some of Lincoln's most profound quotes, such as "There is nothing stronger than gentleness," became hallmarks of my father's. In fact, I think I first came to understand the idea that mentorship was a chain of sharing by learning from my father's own interest in Lincoln. Because my father found him such an inspiring figure, he sought to incorporate lessons from the president's life into his own; because I admired my father so much, I absorbed many of his traits in my own life. Thus the legacy of Lincoln was passed on from my father's studies to me.

I REALLY CAME to know Lincoln for myself while I was in college. A librarian at Purdue named Blanche Miller noticed that I kept checking out books on the president. She started to make suggestions to me about new books on Lincoln, or older ones I might not have come across. It was so exciting for me to delve into the complex mind and philosophy of a political figure such as Lincoln, because it was so separate from my athletic life and schoolwork—but it also gave me a feeling of familiarity, since I knew my father had read many of the same books and even pondered some of the same lessons.

One of the first things that stood out to me about Lincoln's life was the way he handled adversity. His mother died while he was still very young. He didn't have consistent access to schooling, so he taught himself. He was defeated in his first attempt at public office. He filed for bankruptcy. He was unlucky in love. He lost three times in his bid for the U.S. Senate. He suffered from what would probably be considered by today's standards to be severe clinical depression. But he persevered. It wasn't just his presidency that interested me; it also was everything he encountered on the road to the presidency that really captured my attention.

Had Lincoln been given the option, he probably would not have selected all of the trials he suffered; but rather than collapsing under their weight, he used them to strengthen himself for his next goal. He was determined to learn from everything that came his way, even if the lesson was painful and the experience heartbreaking. "I do not think much of a man who is not wiser today than he was yesterday," he once remarked. To him, life was a series of lessons that presented opportunities. Wisdom came from making the most of each one.

It seems to me that had Lincoln not gone through all of the disappointments he did before he became the commander in chief, he would not have been adequately prepared to preside during arguably the most tumultuous period of American history. Because he had not been spared the harsh realities of life—the heartaches and the disappointments—he could deal with the larger trials that awaited him down the road.

Lincoln himself once said, "The worst things you can do for those you love are the things they could and should do for themselves." He fiercely believed in self-sufficiency, and in the maturity and character that struggles and hardships can bring. This lesson is so important for teachers and parents. It is only natural for us to want to shield our students and our children from anything that might possibly cause them hurt or to suffer or even to be uncomfortable. But some degree of pain is necessary for a person to become suited for the responsibilities that lay ahead.

I remember feeling awed when I first realized the scope of his early disappointments. It was 1928, my senior year of high school, and I felt a camaraderie with the young man who would go on to be president. The sad story of his life stayed with me over the next few years. While I had little adversity in my young life—I was privileged enough to be enrolled in college, still had two loving parents, and was courting my one true love—I didn't have to look very far to see examples of this kind of fortitude in those around me. My father, of course, came immediately to mind. The setbacks and losses in his own life were great, but he used them to move forward rather than as excuses to throw in the towel.

Lincoln also modeled how to move past disappointments without carrying grudges. The famous closing remarks of his second inaugural address still move me, as he urged Americans:

> With malice toward none, with charity for all, with firmness in the right as God gives us to see the right, let us strive on to finish the work we are in, to bind up the nation's wounds, to care for him who shall have borne the battle and for his widow and his orphan, to do all which may achieve and cherish a just and lasting peace among ourselves and with all nations.

"With malice toward none"—what a noble goal for us all to hold in our lives! The country was in the midst of an internal conflict that tore apart families, that tore the very fabric of our nation apart at the seams; yet Lincoln's concern was that no one should carry resentment, grudges, or ill will toward his neighbors for any disagreement.

He was standing as the commander in chief of an army

locked in battle, but he did not draw strength from the clashes or confidence from the victories. Instead, he grieved over every loss; each fallen soldier pained him, no matter the color of his uniform. Lincoln understood that the Confederate Army was defending its homeland and rights as they saw fit, and he mourned that the political situation had made battle necessary to resolve the conflict. He did not savor victories by the Union troops, except insofar as each one might be a step toward ending the war.

That shows a capacity for compassion that is, perhaps, larger than most of us could muster; and yet, what an incredible lesson in forgiveness and reconciliation. How many of us have conflicts with someone else—and how many of us pray for that person? We have individuals with whom we are competitive, or whom we dislike or have a quarrel with; but very few of us have true enemies in the martial sense. And yet if Lincoln could pray fervently—and contemporary reports indicate he did—for the people who were opposing him, how much more can we do for someone we just find a little irritating?

In the Gospel of Matthew, Christians are instructed to Love your enemies and pray for those who persecute you. I have always found this one of the hardest passages in Scripture to live by, but Lincoln showed me that it could be done. Similarly, in Romans 12:20, Scripture says, "If your enemy is hungry, feed him; if he is thirsty, give him something to drink. In doing this, you will heap burning coals on his head." That line always kind of stuck in my craw when I was younger. I couldn't imagine how it would be possible to go out of my way to show kindness to someone with whom I had a major disagreement. It seemed to go against human nature.

But Lincoln showed exactly how to follow such a command when he was questioned on his reparations and reconstruction policy for the South, which many Northern lawmakers saw as far too generous. When they protested that he was supposed to destroy his enemies rather than to befriend them, Lincoln famously answered, "Am I not destroying my enemies when I make friends of them?"

That response—its wisdom and temperance—shakes me to my core every time I read it. Holding on to old grudges and nursing wounds we refuse to allow to heal can keep us locked in the same place. More than once in my life, I found myself wanting to point a finger at my critics and give them a piece of my mind, such as when annoyed fans from other schools would send hateful mail, or when sportswriters would take jabs at UCLA's program—but what would that accomplish? Nothing. It would only give them more reason to dislike me. Lincoln's example of reaching out to former enemies through acts of compassion made me radically reconsider the way I reacted toward those opposed to me.

Perhaps the most incredible example of Lincoln's wisdom in this realm can be seen in the people with whom he chose to surround himself. I pride myself on having read just about every major book ever published about Abraham Lincoln, but the one that has affected me the most in recent years is Doris Kearns Goodwin's exceptional text *Team of Rivals*. In this book, Goodwin examines in profound depth a well-documented but not widely discussed political decision: When Lincoln was elected to the presidency, he appointed a number of former political opponents to serve as his advisers and to fill various posts.

In a move that fascinated me from the time I first read of it, Lincoln even offered the command of the U.S. Army to Robert E. Lee in 1861. The president knew that Lee was fiercely loyal to Virginia, but also that he held a deep dislike for the secession movement and was morally opposed to slavery. Though some of Lincoln's allies would question the move, Lincoln believed that engaging a good man with ties to the opposing force would go a long way in placating the surging tide of conflict.

Lee, of course, declined the offer, though he did so with a heavy heart. He felt that his loyalty ultimately lay with the government of his home state. But Lincoln's gesture was a significant one, and the respect between two men who should have been bitter enemies remained throughout their lifetimes.

Lincoln's philosophy of reaching across traditional boundaries was unconventional, to say the least; many people viewed it as shocking, disturbing, or even foolhardy. But Lincoln was no fool. By selecting men whom he knew disagreed with him or differed from his own platform, he assured himself of several things. First, he would be confronted with legitimate challenges to his ideas, rather than finding himself in a pool of yesmen. This meant that his policies would emerge more clearly reasoned and justified.

Second, he recognized that an enemy drawn into his fold would be more likely to become an ally because of mutual respect. He relied on loyalty and honor to keep those former rivals from acting in an underhanded manner. Thus he protected himself from political attacks from those who might be jockeying for power against him; he also shrank the pool of adversaries working against his interests.

Several times during my career I found myself facing a difficult situation with a member of my coaching staff. Before I go any farther, I have to take a moment to say how very blessed I was in my career; over the years, I had the privilege of working with the most amazing and talented staffs ever assembled in college basketball. I was able to recruit and maintain a number of tremendous men who just as easily could have been head coaches at almost any other university, but who chose to stay with our team at UCLA because they believed in how we operated and what we stood for.

However, there were times when we differed on strategy or game philosophy. Those disagreements never got heated, but sometimes they were very intense. Just as I imagine Lincoln would have been, I was pleased when those challenges arose because it meant that my fellow coaches were as passionate about our team as I was. Nothing ruins a team more quickly than apathy. And besides, if there were never any disagreement, you wouldn't need an assistant.

Lincoln sought not only diverse opinions and advice when he brought in his former rivals; he also sought men who had vision and strong beliefs so that together they could harness their energies for a common purpose. Each man might hold an ardent belief in something different—if not different in issue, then different in solution. But it was this zeal that each man brought that would unite them.

Based on Lincoln's example, I encouraged my assistant coaches to speak up with ideas that might differ from or even completely contradict my own. We would debate these issues, and I would ask for input from everyone. If I decided in the end to go with a new suggestion, we'd all forge ahead together and see how it worked.

If we succeeded, I always tried to remember who had offered the idea in the first place and to praise him when talking to the media. After all, he had been the one to think innovatively and suggest bravely. One assistant suggested that we bring back a zone press. We'd used it a few years previously but had phased it out. When we resurrected it at the assistant's suggestion, it ended up taking us to our first National Championship, in 1964. I really tried to make a point of praising him to the press after that event because he'd had the courage to suggest something outside the status quo.

On the other hand, if a suggestion did not succeed, I always tried to forget who had made the suggestion. After all, as the

Joshua Wooden,
John Wooden's father

John Wooden and Nellie Riely

Glenn Curtis

Ward "Piggy" Lambert

Abraham Lincoln

Mother Teresa

Coach and
Kareem Abdul-
Jabbar (formerly
Lewis Alcindor)

Bill Walton
and Coach

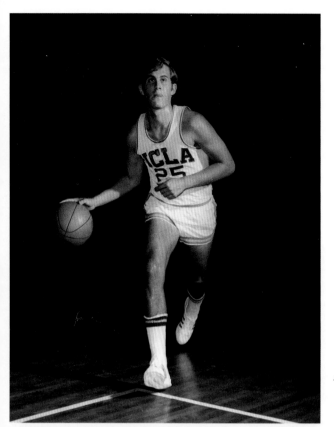

Andy Hill

Bob Vigars

Roy Williams and Coach

Dale Brown and Coach

Coach with great-granddaughter
Cori Nicholson, when she was small

John and Nellie Wooden

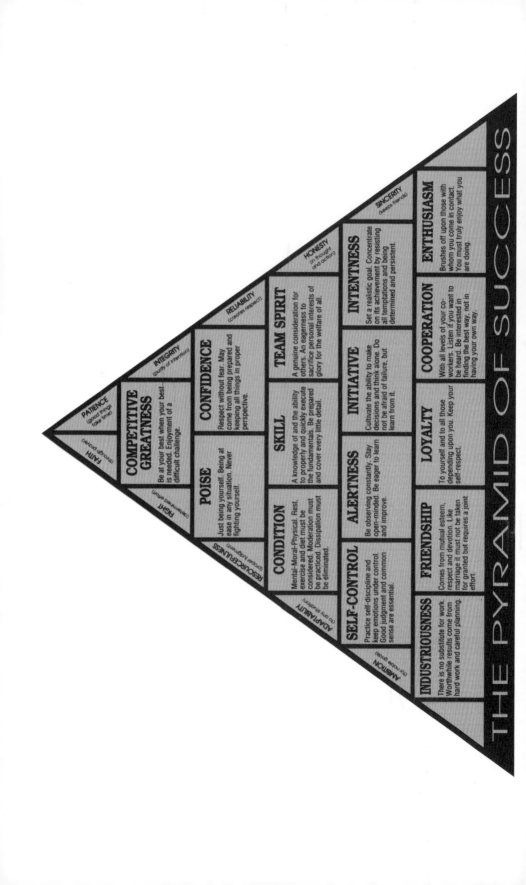

THE PYRAMID OF SUCCESS

ENTHUSIASM — Brushes off upon those with whom you come in contact. You must truly enjoy what you are doing.

SINCERITY (keeps friends)

INTENTNESS — Set a realistic goal. Concentrate on its achievement by resisting all temptations and being determined and persistent.

HONESTY (in thought and action)

TEAM SPIRIT — A genuine consideration for others. An eagerness to sacrifice personal interests of glory for the welfare of all.

RELIABILITY (creates respect)

CONFIDENCE — Respect without fear. May come from being prepared and keeping all things in proper perspective.

INTEGRITY (purity of intention)

COMPETITIVE GREATNESS — Be at your best when your best is needed. Enjoyment of a difficult challenge.

PATIENCE (good things take time)

FAITH (through prayer)

POISE — Just being yourself. Being at ease in any situation. Never fighting yourself.

RIGHT (determined effort)

SKILL — A knowledge of and the ability to properly and quickly execute the fundamentals. Be prepared and cover every little detail.

INITIATIVE — Cultivate the ability to make decisions and think alone. Do not be afraid of failure, but learn from it.

COOPERATION — With all levels of your co-workers. Listen if you want to be heard. Be interested in finding the best way, not in having your own way.

ALERTNESS — Be observing constantly. Stay open-minded. Be eager to learn and improve.

LOYALTY — To yourself and to all those depending upon you. Keep your self-respect.

CONDITION — Mental-Moral-Physical. Rest, exercise and diet must be considered. Moderation must be practiced. Dissipation must be eliminated.

RESOURCEFULNESS (proper judgment)

SELF-CONTROL — Practice self-discipline and keep emotions under control. Good judgment and common sense are essential.

ADAPTABILITY (to any situation)

FRIENDSHIP — Comes from mutual esteem, respect and devotion. Like marriage it must not be taken for granted but requires a joint effort.

INDUSTRIOUSNESS — There is no substitute for work. Worthwhile results come from hard work and careful planning.

AMBITION (for noble goals)

head coach, I had ultimately been the one who made the deci-sion and the call. Besides, if you call attention to failed ideas by assigning blame rather than accepting it, you discourage peo-ple from making suggestions the next time around.

Only once during my career did I find myself at odds with an assistant to the extent that the situation was irreconcilable. Fortunately, that assistant chose to leave our staff before the situation worsened. He ended up having a successful career in another field, and I was genuinely happy for him. Given the countless personality traits and motives an individual can pos-sess, I think it's a pretty remarkable statistic that only one man among dozens I hired proved to be an obstacle too tough to tackle with respect, interest, and gentle leadership. If it worked with the vast majority of my assistant coaches, I think that's a pretty good testimony to the power of the idea. I think Lincoln would be pleased.

ONE OF THE main reasons why this philosophy works, I think, is that at its core is genuine concern and regard for the other par-ties. Lincoln truly cared about the opinions of his comrades, and he truly cared about the outcomes of their discussions. But further, he treated them with respect so that they would con-tinue to offer those opinions. Lincoln's genuine concern, for both issues and people, demonstrated that it is a common trait among those who would seek to be strong mentors.

That was what I sought when I began to study the life and writings of Abraham Lincoln in the Purdue University library nearly eighty years ago. I wasn't looking for what could help me in history class. I wasn't nearly as curious about the man who had changed the course of American history as I was about the man who had inspired my father—the mentor of my mentor. That was the Lincoln I sought to know. And in the course of trying to learn more about what had made my father so great, I discovered a man who would serve as a mentor in my own life as well.

If mentoring is a kind of parenting, then I suppose it can produce grandchildren, too. Mentoring can create generations—the lessons learned from one individual are incorporated in a life that then teaches its principles to another. I learned from Lincoln what my father had learned from him. To outward appearances, they were very different men: one a statesman, the other a farmer. But their humility, modest roots, temperate lifestyles, and gentleness of spirit formed a bond between them, even though they lived generations apart.

And in my own time, I came to understand that a mentor can speak across time and place, teaching truths through the decisions of his own life and the thoughts of his own pen. The legacy a person leaves with his or her actions and writings is no less a means of mentoring than is a one-on-one conversation about experience and advice.

The example Lincoln forged with his life and letters granted me not only a mentor of character, but also a lesson in the limitless nature of mentoring. That a man I never met could shape my thinking so profoundly also taught me that my words on paper and my life in the media could reach far more people than those with whom I have personally interacted. Not all of us will have the chance to write books or speak on camera or have our lives researched by interested students; but we can all be mentors, and in so doing, collectively shape the character of our nation as much as its most visible leaders.

DURING MY LIFETIME I've been blessed to have a number of awards presented to me. I don't really have very many of the ones from the past twenty years or so put up in my home. There is one exception: In 2003, President Bush invited me to the White House to award me the Presidential Medal of Honor, the nation's highest civilian honor.

Shortly after he handed me this medal, one of my former players, who had made the trip with me, noted that the entire ceremony had taken place in the room where Lincoln lay in state. His death was tragic, but his life was tremendous. And as I held that medal, I was overcome with a profound sense of gratitude toward Lincoln and all the mentors who had forged me into the man I had become.

CHAPTER 8

· · · · · · · · · · · ·

My Beloved Nellie

People tend to throw out a lot of numbers when they talk about my life: almost thirty years as a college head coach, ten National Championships in twelve years, a 671–161 win-loss record. But all of those numbers pale in comparison to the number of which I am the most proud: *one.*

My Nellie was the one and only woman I ever loved, ever kissed, ever hoped to share a life with. And even though she passed away in 1985 after fifty-three years of marriage, my love for her remains as strong as it ever was. I still keep her pajamas laid out on her side of the bed, and I've written a letter to her every single month on the date of her passing. She was my strength and encouragement, my comfort and my support—she taught me so much about love. But she taught me more than that, too. The one woman for me also mentored me in the importance of trust.

Even from our first real conversation, Nellie was teaching me this important lesson. It started the summer after my freshman year in high school. I was out plowing in the fields when I saw a car pull up with some girls and a boy inside. They climbed out and went up to the fence, calling to me, but I just kept on plowing, and finally they went away. I hadn't meant to be rude; I knew those kids. I'd seen them around town and I happened to think that one of the girls was just about the prettiest thing I'd ever laid eyes on. But here I was covered in dirt and sweat and blisters, and I hardly imagined she'd think much of that.

Once school started up again, that girl and I had home room together, and on the very first day back she stopped me and asked, "Why didn't you come over to talk to us when we drove all the way up there to see you?"

I told her the truth: "I was dirty and perspiring and you would have made fun of me."

She got a very serious look on her face and said, "Oh, no, John, I would *never* make fun of you."

And that was the moment I fell in love with my Nellie.

THE REASON THAT story has stayed with me wasn't just that it was my first real contact with the woman I'd love for the rest of my life. Like all good lessons, it took on more significance as time went on. When a fourteen-year-old Nellie told me, "I would *never* make fun of you," she was giving me the first in a series of lessons she'd teach me throughout the rest of her life: Trust people to do the right thing.

Trust is not an easy lesson to learn; in fact, it's often one that people learn as a result of experiencing the *betrayal* of trust first. I don't think there's a person on Earth who can't empathize with the horrible sinking in your stomach when you realize that someone you trusted has betrayed you. Perhaps the only feeling worse than that is the sickening realization that you've betrayed the trust someone has given you.

Conversely, there is hardly a better feeling in the world than knowing that you've been entrusted with a major assignment at work, with a responsibility to your team, or with the heart of another person. Trust means that someone else recognizes and values your abilities, your spirit, and your integrity. It is more than just a compliment to your skill; it is a testament to your character that you have been deemed trustworthy.

As I came to discover throughout my career, this feeling of trust is essential in any meaningful relationship. It is essential for players to trust their coaches, and it is essential for coaches to trust their players. In fact, any teacher-student relationship is built on a kind of mutual trust: The student trusts the teacher to share knowledge, and the teacher trusts the student to use that knowledge in the best possible way. It is essential both to trust and to be trustworthy, and no one taught me that better than Nellie. Every facet of her character seemed to offer a lesson in trust: trust in her kindness, trust in her judgment, trust in her ability, trust in her character, trust in her love, and trust in her faith in me.

When I left for college, Nellie still had one more year of high school to complete, and after that she worked in Martinsville while I finished up my time at Purdue. We weren't married until after basketball season my senior year of college, and the wait sometimes seemed too much.

I never dated anyone else; Nellie was the only girl for me. But I know it was tough for her just to sit at home and pine for me—she was lively and outgoing, and she loved to be in a crowd, so she eventually started to go out on dates. I call them dates because that's what they felt like to me, but I know she wasn't serious about any of those guys, and she certainly wasn't looking to start a relationship. She was just looking for some-one to take her dancing. Nellie loved dancing; she couldn't get enough of it. I, however, couldn't be bothered with it. Maybe I was too serious, or too shy, or too awkward—I'm not quite sure. But she always wanted to go out dancing when I was home, and I just never had the desire.

As I started reading her letters about the groups she was going out with and the boys she was dancing with, I got jealous. Very jealous. There were a number of girls at Purdue who tried to catch my eye (though I'm sure it was more because of my basketball uniform than anything), but I never went beyond a polite "Hello" because I had only one girl on my mind. The problem was, I couldn't stand the thought of my girl being out with other people while I stayed holed up in a dormitory.

Nellie and I finally talked about it during one of my visits home. "John," she said in that same serious tone she used in our very first conversation, "you're the only man I love and the only man I want to marry. You're going to have to trust me that I am true to you."

It was such a simple statement, but it was so true. Here, I had been so jealous over something I thought she was doing, when deep down I knew the problem was that I wasn't giving her enough credit. That's not to say it was an easy fix. Quite the opposite—I struggled for years with jealousy. But I finally learned that for a relationship to be a full connection forged from mutual respect, I had to fully trust her and to *let her know* that I fully trusted her. Otherwise the relationship would remain focused on "me" and what I was feeling rather than how we came together as individuals to create a "we."

TRUST CAN TAKE many forms. In a relationship, it's not just about learning to trust someone else's actions or intentions. It's also about trusting him or her to think of both of you before acting. The only real disagreement Nellie and I had in all our years of marriage came when I enlisted in the Navy in 1942. I didn't ask her first—I just went down to the recruiting office and joined, then told her about it afterward. She wasn't too happy with me, but her reason for being upset wasn't that she didn't want me to serve. She just didn't like the fact that I hadn't bothered to talk to her first, especially because I had been afraid that she'd be opposed to my enlisting.

By enlisting behind her back, I hadn't demonstrated that I trusted her enough to be able to discuss the situation rationally and to recognize when there was something I felt I had to act on. I think she was hurt more than she was upset, and it was yet another reminder to me of why trust is essential in making relationships work. She supported me, though, during my service through the war. When it was over and I was unemployed because my old teaching job was filled by someone else, she never panicked, but trusted me to find a way to provide for our family.

I COULD ALWAYS trust Nellie to be a source of support for me in a variety of ways. When I was first teaching high school, we didn't have the facilities to get our athletic equipment and uniforms cleaned between practices. I talked to Nellie about the frustrations that caused and then asked her a huge favor: Would she be willing to wash the team's laundry? It was a lot for me to ask of her, but she agreed without complaining. Every evening I'd bring home a load of socks, jerseys, jockstraps, and shorts, and every morning she would have a stack of clean ones folded and ready for practice that afternoon.

I was so grateful to her, not only because she was doing so much work on the team's behalf, but also because she had shown me that I could trust her to support what I needed to get done to do my job more effectively. She had always been my biggest fan and my most enthusiastic supporter, but I guess

I never realized just how strong her devotion really was until I saw how readily she accepted the task I asked of her. With every uniform she washed, she was showing me that I could trust her to be a partner to me.

Some people may be offended by this story—I was off at my job and expected my wife to do the laundry for a whole bunch of boys who weren't even her children. But that's not how Nellie saw it, and it's not how I see it either. She and I had an understanding about our roles in the marriage: I would work to bring home a paycheck in whatever way I had to (which even included working for a local dairy in the mornings before my teaching job started), and Nellie would manage our home in a way that would allow me to continue earning money to support her and our children.

We trusted each other to fulfill those roles because if either of us slipped, the balance would be broken and our family would suffer. We each depended on the other and trusted each other to do what needed to be done. When I asked Nellie to do the extra washing, she had every right and reason to say, "Are you crazy, John? No way!" But by taking it on, she was really saying, "I love you and I trust that you are asking me to do what you need done for your work so you can continue to support our family."

Nellie never complained about the long hours and scant pay I made as a teacher and a coach. The jobs didn't pay much and usually didn't come with any kind of retirement plan, and the travel to away games was sometimes very strenuous. And yet she never once showed any apprehension about having enough to feed ourselves and our children, and she never complained about not having any luxuries. Instead, she trusted me to provide for the family, and the faith she showed in my ability to do that only made me a better provider.

She also never complained that my job moved us around

quite a bit. When a new opportunity arose, we would talk it over, and if we determined together that it was in our family's best interest that I take the job, we went forward with it. She always trusted that we would make it all work out in the end.

Nothing illustrates this better than our move to California. When both the University of Minnesota and UCLA extended job offers to me in 1948, Nell and I agreed that Minnesota would be our top choice because it would keep us closer to our families in the Midwest. I'd asked Minnesota if I could choose my own assistant coaching staff and they weren't sure about it at first, but promised they would call me by six P.M. on Sunday with their decision. When six came and went without a call, Nellie and I both figured that they must have rejected my request. At seven, UCLA called, and we accepted their offer, not knowing that a blizzard had knocked out the wires in the Twin Cities, preventing Minnesota from calling to let me know they'd agreed to my terms. They finally reached me at about seven-thirty, but by then I'd made my promise to the Bruins.

So it was with some reservations that we headed west that summer, feeling nervous and unsure about how we'd do living on the West Coast. And the transition wasn't easy. It took several years before we all felt really at home there—Los Angeles was quite a bit different from anywhere in Indiana. But despite the adjustment struggles, Nellie never made me second-guess myself, and she never complained about the decision we'd made. She had an amazing amount of trust in me, that I was doing what was best for the family and that I was living as a man of my word. I had trust in her that she would continue to raise our children and create a loving home wherever my job took us. The knowledge of that trust really helped me through our adjustment period in California.

————————

Her unwavering confidence in me showed me how to trust my teams to make the most of their skills and to play with integrity. My players felt that trust, I know, and I think it made them a stronger team. My confidence in them made them confident in themselves. I tried to emphasize to them the importance of trusting their own instincts and trusting their fellow players to react wisely in any game scenario. Nellie's example pervaded my coaching from my first team right to my last one—and what a lesson in trust that last one was!

Maybe the most remarkable way Nellie was a mentor to me with regard to trust was in the way she handled my retirement announcement. I had never really discussed it with her, and I hadn't even given it that much thought myself. We'd agreed that we'd somehow just know when the time was right, and that time came when we beat Louisville to go to the NCAA finals for the 1974–75 tournament. It was an incredibly close game and either team could have won or lost it. (But, of course, the right team won!)

It was a beautiful game. Both teams played outstanding ball, and it was shame that one had to lose. A Louisville player missed a foul shot in regulation that almost surely would have won the game for them. This player had a perfect season at free throws until he missed this one; they were leading by two, and he missed the first half of the one-and-one. We got the ball, scored, and tied the game (back then, they didn't have a three-point shot). And then things just went our way in overtime, and we won the game.

I was excited and I was proud and then, as I was walking across the gymnasium to the press room, as I'd done hundreds of times before, I suddenly realized that I just didn't want to face the reporters. It was the strangest feeling; I simply found my mind telling me, "It's time now."

I went to the locker room first. The players were getting ready to shower, and I called them together and praised them for a wonderful game. I knew we were looking ahead to a tough matchup in the finals, though, with a Kentucky team that boasted some of the tallest players in college basketball that year. Then I told them very simply, "I don't know how we'll do Monday night against Kentucky, but fellows, I know we're quicker, and I believe you've got enough size among you to counter their height.

"But regardless of how the game turns out I want you players to know I've never had a team in all my years that I've enjoyed more. There isn't any player on the team this year who has given me any trouble on or off the court. And that's a pretty nice thing to say about the last team I'll ever teach."

My players were surprised; my assistants were shocked. But I wanted them to hear it from me first, and I wanted them to know how proud I was to be retiring with that team. And then I went to face the press. I knew someone in the press room was bound to ask me about retirement, since I would be sixty-five by the start of the next season—and sure enough, the question came up.

I didn't have a chance to see Nellie until after we were dressed and leaving the gym—and it definitely crossed my mind how she'd reacted when I joined the Navy, which was the last time I'd made a major career decision without telling her first. But I also knew that we'd grown since then and that the decision was one we both knew was coming and that it needed to happen at the right time. And somehow I just knew this was the right time.

Sure enough, Nellie was okay with the news when I told her. In fact, she was excited, giving me a big hug and kiss. She trusted me to know when it was right, and I'd learned enough about trust from her by then to know that. I think just knowing that she would support my decision, whenever and however it came, helped me to realize it was time to go forward. And I'll say this: I never regretted it. Not for one second.

We went on to beat Kentucky in the final game, 92–85, and sealed our tenth National Championship in twelve years—a wonderful end to a wonderful career. But I had to laugh as I continued to think about Nellie's reaction. After all this time, she was still teaching me to trust, which just served to remind me, even as I was supposedly retiring from teaching, that I should never really leave it behind.

SHE AND I were baptized together in 1927, but her faith was always years ahead of mine. She trusted God like no one else I knew. She never swerved and could never be shaken from her belief. She had a resoluteness about her trust in Him that amazed me. When something was challenging us, she would pray for acceptance, trusting that God would work it out for the best. When we ended up in California rather than Minnesota and she had some trouble getting used to life out there, rather than complaining, she put her trust in God that He had led us where He wanted us to be and would direct our paths from there.

She had a flip book of various inspirational sayings, and she would turn to a new one each morning. The last one she turned to before she passed away was a simple prayer: "I pray thee, O God, that I may be beautiful within." That statement, beyond anything else, truly epitomizes her spirit and her lifelong trust in God, through His love, to always work on us all. She took the idea of love through action very seriously.

I remember one evening, when we were still a young couple, Nellie looked at me very seriously and said, "John, I want us to make love every single day of our marriage. And I don't mean that sexually—it can be a look or a touch or a kind word or an action. I mean that I want us to actually create love in our home each and every day of our lives."

That was one of the simplest and most profound ideas I had ever heard. That's exactly what Nellie sought to do, and I found that the love she created was a blessing to our family, and to other people as well. She was an amazing mother to our own children, of course, but she was also a mother away from home for my players, and they all came to love her like one. She would cook a huge meal and invite my team over for dinner at least three or four times every season. She offered my players advice and hugs and even a kick in the pants if they needed it. She brought such an attitude of caring to the team that I was continually amazed by her untiring enthusiasm and support for all of us.

Her trust in God's work was well placed—Nellie had one of the most beautiful spirits I have ever been blessed to encounter, and as she continually sought to live her faith through love, she continued to teach me in ways she probably never fully knew.

When I was courting her, we spent a great deal of time listening to music on her family's Victrola. There were two records in particular that we listened to over and over again: "Ramona" and "In a Little Spanish Town." Nellie was always trying to get me to dance with her when they played, and it was a rare evening when I could actually be persuaded to join her; but I can still hear the music of those songs and I can still sing the words. There is one line in particular from "Ramona" that really comes to mind when I think about Nellie: "I press you, caress you / And bless the day you taught me to care." That is really what was so remarkable about her—she managed to teach me with the way she lived her life. Like the Ramona of the song, Nellie taught me to care not just for her, but to allow my care to take the form of trust in other people. She showed me how important trust is, and how to live life as a person worthy of receiving trust.

And it's a lesson in mentoring for which I will always be grateful.

PART II

· · · · · · ·

Seven People to Whom
I Have Been a Mentor

CHAPTER 9

· · · · · · · · · · ·

Pay It Forward

THE AMAZING LESSONS I'VE LEARNED from my seven mentors have not been solely mine. In fact, I've made it my job
to share those lessons . . . because that's what we should do.

As much as this is a book written in honor of my personal
mentors, I also am writing this in tribute to seven other people.
They are people who have told me or told others that I have
been a mentor to them.

There is six-time NBA champion Kareem Abdul-Jabbar, who
also was a great Bruin when we knew him as Lewis Alcindor.
I've also been called a mentor by NBA Hall of Famer Bill Walton,
who broke a few of Alcindor's records when he played at UCLA.
Both had incredible careers as players and role models for as-
piring athletes. And there is Andy Hill, a man I recruited and
who was on some of our great teams during his UCLA career.
Unlike Bill and Kareem, Andy wasn't an All-American. In fact,
he barely ever played. But our relationship, rekindled a little
over a decade ago, is true testament to the power of mentoring.

And there are coaches, too, who have shaped the lives and careers of countless players—coaches such as Roy Williams at the
University of North Carolina, who has more than five hundred

college victories in his career and whose team won the National Championship in 2005 and 2009; and Dale Brown from Louisiana State University, who led the Tigers for a full quarter of a century and was named the college coach of the year twice.

And there are people I've never met, such as Bob Vigars, a special education teacher and basketball coach from St. Thomas, Ontario, Canada. Men such as Bob have done me the greatest honor and handed me the most serious responsibility a person can possibly be given—they named me as a mentor in their own lives, even though we've never met.

Finally, there is my great-granddaughter, Cori Nicholson, who has earned her college degree and is now a kindergarten teacher in California. She said she pursued this route because she loved to watch me teach.

The knowledge that these seven individuals look to me for advice and guidance and encouragement and teaching inspires me to live each day in a manner that is worthy of this great honor. I do not accept this responsibility lightly, and I am aware every day of the lives that each of these individuals will influence with their own living. Therefore they are also my mentors, and I also write this book for them.

CHAPTER 10

Kareem Abdul-Jabbar

Some people who know a little about the championships our teams won at UCLA think that our string of wins began when Lewis Alcindor, an amazing seven-foot-one high school player from New York, chose to become a Bruin. Actually, our teams won championships in the two years before Lewis arrived, but he certainly changed the landscape, both for us and for college basketball. Lewis— he would later change his name to Kareem Abdul-Jabbar, but I have always called him Lewis—taught me many lessons in his four years at UCLA. I learned how to make changes to our offensive structure to account for his great gifts and size. I had never had a player his size before, so I learned to adapt in ways that were new. He was so different that he made every opponent change their game at each end of the court. He also was a great thinker. I so enjoyed our conversations about literature, conversations I didn't have with some others. And finally, he showed as much self-control as I had seen since watching my own father handle challenges as I was growing up. Like my father, Lewis never complained or made excuses, no matter

*the situation. While with Lewis, I learned more about
man's inhumanity to man than from anyone else. People
made terrible remarks within his earshot. I must say, I'm
not sure that if I had been placed in his position, I would
have taken it the way he did. Yet despite the things others
said or did, he always managed his own behavior in ways
that would make any parent—or mentor—proud. There
are not many people I've compared favorably to my father,
but I know he would be proud to have Lewis on that list.*

—John Wooden

· · · · · · · ·

IT WAS MARCH 21, 1964, AND I HAD been invited, along with a
number of my high school friends, to attend the Saturday
evening birthday party for one of our classmates. Though I was
only a junior, I was considered one of the best high school basketball players in the country, so my passion for the game was
well known—especially by our host. As the party progressed,
her father invited me and a few others into the bedroom, where
he had his television set tuned to that night's college basketball
National Championship game.

I had heard about the team from UCLA because they were a
pretty good story. The Bruins had won all twenty-nine games
they had played coming into the game and had done so with a
team that many writers called undersized. Duke, on the other
hand, had two six-foot-ten-inch players—Hack Tison and Jay
Buckley. UCLA ran Duke ragged and won the title game, 93–83.
By winning, they completed only the third undefeated season
in Division I college basketball history at the time.

A year later, I was invited to the same birthday party—and
again ended up in the bedroom watching the National Championship game. And again, UCLA's smaller team ran another

big-time opponent into the ground. Behind forty-two points from Gail Goodrich, the Bruins beat the Michigan Wolverines, 91–80. Not a single starter on UCLA's team was taller than six-foot-five.

As I watched those games I couldn't help but wonder what it would be like to play for Coach Wooden and UCLA. I loved their style, their press, their approach to the game. I knew I could fit, even though some might look at my height and wonder why I could say that so confidently. To many basketball fans, I wasn't the "big man" they expected from someone more than seven feet tall. At the time, the pro game was being dominated by Wilt Chamberlain and Bill Russell, big guys who were tall and broad-shouldered. I was too thin, some said, and played with too much finesse.

But that was exactly why I believed I could fit into the UCLA style of offense and defense, which depended on speed and quickness more than brutish strength. John Wooden believed the same thing. And when I told him I wanted to study at UCLA, I had no idea how much I would learn.

EDUCATION HAS ALWAYS played a prominent role in my life. I was fortunate that my parents, Al and Cora Alcindor, placed an emphasis on it from a very early age. It was more than mere coincidence that I was surrounded by books and music in our home as a child.

Yet I really grew as a student and a scholar-athlete at UCLA under Coach Wooden's guidance. Much of what I know—what made me a smart man—has come from John Wooden.

I knew very quickly that Coach Wooden would be a mentor to me. I was an English major, and obviously he was an English teacher, so often on road trips we would find ourselves in conversations in which I would be asking him questions about the use of a colon versus a semicolon, or the use of certain prepositions or other words. It was a different kind of relationship than I think I imagined, but it was based on a mutual love for language. He would share poems with me that meant a lot to him. I shared several with him that were meaningful to me, and he would look up those poems and learn from them. It was special, and a primary reason I always speak of the privilege of playing for him.

He was a person who cared and who taught proper values. And he was always genuine about it. He got rich from it—not in material wealth, but he got rich from it nonetheless. It boggles your mind to think what he would be worth in today's market. As a coach, he would be paid millions. But his value as an educator is priceless.

It's one of the reasons I chose UCLA coming out of New York City's Power Memorial High in 1965. I was impressed with how Coach Wooden stressed academics and wanted all of his players to graduate. Even as I was closing on the end of my UCLA career, keenly aware that a promising professional basketball career was in front of me, the importance of my education never waned.

It had been instilled in me since my childhood that I should value education; but also, Coach Wooden constantly emphasized "finishing things you started." Certain basketball stardom or not, I was determined to earn my degree.

And I did.

OF COURSE, MY parents were instrumental in fostering an educational environment. I was raised in Manhattan's Dyckman Street projects, a multiethnic, middle-class enclave that gave me an enduring awareness of how big the world was and how wide the range of human experience could be.

Beyond the cultural diversity of the neighborhood, I was surrounded by books and music at home. My father, Al, attended Juilliard School of Music, served in the Army, and was a longtime police officer with the New York City Transit Authority. A musician who jammed with Thelonius Monk, he shared his love for jazz with me, further opening my mind. He was the strong, silent type, but music brought out his personality. My mother, Cora, was more outspoken but probably a bit overprotective of her only child.

Initially I attended P.S. 52, where I was first introduced to the game of basketball. I remember the five-story, redbrick building with two large doors, right off the street at ground level, leading straight up to the gymnasium, where I picked up my first basketball the summer between first and second grades. I spent a lot of time there trying to muster the strength to get the ball to the basket as a young boy. Eventually I moved over to St. Jude's, where I began the Catholic school education that carried me through my years at Power Memorial. At St. Jude's I began to blossom as a student in a disciplined environment, and I also began to grow, not only in stature, but also on the basketball court and in terms of self-confidence.

Learning and fundamentals were part of my life from a very early age. When I was just in fifth grade, my elementary school coach had me working on "George Mikan drills," going to either side of the basket with both hands as the pro game's dominant big man, Mikan, had become famous for doing.

As a ninth grader, I had drawn a lot of attention, and the next year I would go by Coach Jack Donahue's office at Power Memorial and he'd have a basket there for letters from colleges who were interested in me. I'd always ask, "Anyone new today?" Finally he looked at me and said, "Don't worry about college. If you want to go to a college and they have a basketball team, don't worry. I know they'll be interested."

At that stage I started looking at schools that interested me instead of focusing on those that were looking at me. College basketball wasn't all over the television then, as it is today. To follow a team you had to go through the box scores in the newspaper. I began doing that most Sundays and noticing teams that were winning and playing impressively. Coach Wooden and the UCLA Bruins were always there.

I was constantly reading and focused on being a student, both in the classroom and of the game. I think this made it easy to become part of what Coach Wooden was building. He was serious when he said that the biggest promise he could make to me wasn't about basketball, but that I could get a great education. That was an extension of what my mother and father, my high school coach, even my grade school coach stressed to me. And that education would extend well beyond the basketball court.

A NUMBER OF factors played into my decision to attend UCLA. It didn't hurt that I had formed a favorable impression based on prominent African Americans who had attended school there. As a big baseball fan, I grew up listening to Brooklyn Dodgers games on the radio with my mother. Jackie Robinson was my hero. I remember seeing Olympic decathlete Rafer Johnson on *The Ed Sullivan Show* and was really impressed that he was on the show not as an athlete but as the UCLA student body president.

Undersecretary Ralph Bunche of the United Nations also encouraged me to take my mind and basketball talents to the school. Those factors all played into my decision. So did basketball, and Coach Wooden's approach to the game.

Some people thought I wanted to go to a school where I could set scoring records, but that wasn't the case at all. I wanted to go where I would learn the game and play on a winning team. I wanted to be able to cut down the nets at the Final Four. That's what I really wanted.

Coach Wooden and UCLA, which had won those championship games in the two years prior to my arrival, provided me with those opportunities.

I'M OFTEN ASKED what I consider my greatest achievement. Winning championships at the high school, college, and NBA levels, establishing records, and collecting MVP honors have all been rewarding. Doing well in school at UCLA, getting published; those are satisfying.

My greatest achievement, however, has been being a successful parent, sending my kids to school. Habiba, Sultana, Kareem, and Amir are all college grads. They understand who they are, where they are, and have made a good statement with their lives. I think that has been the best thing I have done.

Any success I've had as a parent is the result of listening to Coach Wooden expand on the lessons I learned from my own parents. I would have not been nearly as successful in that area of life if I had not played for Coach, because I learned from him the one thing that made him special as a coach and as a man: He was consistent. That is what he asked of us as players and as a team, and that is the way he coached and taught us. We understood what was expected, and we understood that this would be expected every time. Applying that great lesson to my life as a parent has been challenging, and I'm sure it was challenging for Coach as well. But when coaches or parents make consistency their foundation, everyone around them becomes more comfortable and everyone around them has a greater opportunity to grow.

Coach really made a connection with me by never asking

us to do something he wasn't willing to do or something he hadn't done when he was younger. I remember walking across campus to class in the mornings and going by the track and seeing him out there working out. He had told us to take care of our bodies. At that time he was in his fifties and could have let things go a little, rested on his laurels. But he didn't because he wanted us to see what he was saying, not just hear it.

It was the same way in practice. Coach Wooden was very demanding, always insisting that we do things the right way. But instead of simply telling us how to do things, he would jump right in and provide examples. He didn't talk about his days as a player, but we all knew. He was quite a star in his day, an All-American.

One of his greatest lessons came from something he did not say. Coach Wooden never mentioned winning. It was always, "Fellas, we've got to play to our best. Let's do that." That's a lot different from saying, "Fellas, we've got to win." A lot different. What mattered most to Coach was the effort you made on the court and in the classroom. What mattered was your behavior, your conduct, your values. Of course, that included a strong work ethic. As I grew to understand, if we made the effort he was talking about, winning would often take care of itself. What a lesson.

UP UNTIL AGE eight, I hadn't really encountered racism, but that changed quickly. My best friend in the projects at the time was white. One day, out of the blue, he struck a nerve with a racial slur: "Hey, nigger, you big jungle nigger!"

I was caught completely off-guard, but somehow managed "Fuck you, milk bottle," as a weak response. We never spoke again.

By the 1960s I had become far more socially aware of racism, even though I was attending predominantly white parochial schools. Growing up in that decade of turbulent race relations had a profound effect on my future, especially when Harlem erupted in riots following the murder of a black student by a white policeman prior to the start of my senior year at Power Memorial.

Moving to Westwood at a time when social activism on campus was near its peak further broadened my perspective. In addition to studying American literature, I immersed myself in the political and cultural scene and became an avid reader of black literature. Between my freshman and sophomore years at UCLA I read Alex Haley's biography of Malcolm X. It marked my first real introduction to the Islamic culture and had a profound impact on my thinking.

So did a very public incident that brought back memories of that racial slur from many years before. Walking into a restaurant with Coach Wooden, I was greeted by a shout from a woman: "Oh, look at the big, black freak."

Sensing my shock at the slur, Coach Wooden did his best to diffuse the situation. Fortunately, I had enough maturity and self-confidence to refrain from responding, even though I was angered.

It wasn't until years later that I realized how absolutely upset he was at the moment. He did such a great job of remaining calm and cool that while I was angry and wanted to be angry, he wanted to teach me that the most important thing I could do right then was to pity her for her ignorance. Coach's ability to work with me and understand how best to turn that moment into a classroom of sorts helped me move past a painful moment.

That was the thing about being mentored by Coach Wooden—you never knew when it could happen, and you never knew what the lesson might be. But one thing was sure: With Coach, there was always a lesson.

I ACTUALLY CONVERTED from Catholicism to Islam as a UCLA student, but it wasn't until I was twenty-four and already established in the NBA that I took the name Kareem Abdul-Jabbar. My decision to convert had to do with me having a moral anchor. It was not political in any way.

After reading Malcolm X's biography, I made it a point to learn more about the Muslim faith and the Black Muslim movement. I was fortunate to live in a dorm down the hall from a couple of young Muslim men who were not from Africa and had come to UCLA to study. In conversations with them about their faith, I learned the truth about the Koran and what it does and doesn't say. I realized that was the faith I wanted to embrace. What turned me off, the more I had the chance to look at it, was the Black Muslim movement. It seemed to me that much of what was being said was racist and, to me, racism in any form was wrong.

Of course, I spoke with Coach Wooden—a man of the highest moral character—about my decision to change faiths. The discussion was more out of respect for him than it was for affirmation. Nevertheless, he was supportive.

The conversation was pure Coach Wooden. He was mostly curious about what Islam was and what it meant to me. He was never judgmental, was never trying to convince me that I wasn't believing the right thing, even though I knew that his Christian beliefs were very important to him. He asked lots of questions, listened intently, and appreciated that I had given the decision much thought. Though he never said so, I think he was relieved that I wasn't joining the Nation of Islam or the Black Muslim movement.

While I was a big fan of boxing growing up and a big fan of Muhammad Ali's, boxing was where that connection ended. I didn't agree with what his religion became to him.

I THINK ALL prominent people, no matter what field they are in, have a responsibility to share their knowledge and allow other people to see how to succeed. That's something Coach Wooden imparted in all who played for him at UCLA. Basketball was just a part of my life, but as a player I learned invaluable lessons from him, most of which were contained in his Pyramid of Success.

I initially remember dismissing the Pyramid handout he provided all his players as being "silly." It looked like nothing more than a collection of words with no recognized order. But the longer I was there, the more sense it made.

One of the advantages of getting older is getting wiser, and in time I've grown to appreciate the pyramid and will tell you today that it has been the foundation for my life's work, on and off the court. Coach's pyramid is compatible with my own philosophy on life: Islam.

In recent years I've been able to delve into my deep fascination with both the African American and Native American cultures. I've enjoyed great satisfaction from my second career as an author of half a dozen books, including *A Season on the Reservation*, which came about after embracing the people on the White Mountain Apache Reservation, where I spent a season as an assistant coach at Alchesay High School.

Black Profiles in Courage, Brothers in Arms, and *On the Shoulders of Giants*—my account of the flowering black culture during the Renaissance in Harlem—afforded me the opportunity to share my passion for seldom-told but no less important moments in black history. I enjoy sharing knowledge, something that's incumbent on every generation, but especially so in the black community, where knowledge has not effectively been passed in written form from generation to generation. I've tried to affect that dynamic through my books, so that succeeding generations can see what I saw and learn what I learned. Much of what I saw and learned came from Coach Wooden. He has often described the mind as a palette, and these titles enabled me to paint important pictures.

The Renaissance was an extraordinary time in Harlem. It was where black musicians and writers migrated. Duke Ellington's was the house band at the Cotton Club, and Cab Calloway, who passed up an invitation to play for the Harlem Globetrotters in 1928 for a musical career, became a legend in the jazz world. Not long ago, in an interview for the Academy of Achievement, I was asked what I might share with a young person who came to me for advice. I think the statement "Knowledge is power" is a very succinct way of getting the message across. You have to know what is right, you have to pursue what is right, and the only way you can know and do these things is to acquire knowledge. Flailing around in the dark does not help anyone.

Twenty years have passed since I walked off the floor for the final time with the Los Angeles Lakers as the NBA's all-time scoring leader and six-time MVP. Retiring then marked the end of a twenty-season run in professional basketball. With all that, I hope that my work after basketball in some way defines me beyond the court. Like Coach Wooden, what happened for me in basketball is what many will remember most. And like Coach Wooden, I hope my true legacy will be much bigger than that.

CHAPTER 11

Bill Walton

After Lewis Alcindor had completed his career at UCLA, I wasn't sure I would ever have a player at the center position quite that dominant again. Then came a young man from San Diego who proved me wrong. While Lewis likely changed the game more than any player of his time, Bill Walton was the most complete player I have ever had the privilege of teaching. If there's a secret to success, it just might be little things done well. I love to see little things done well. That was Bill's greatest strength as a player and as a leader. Bill not only made everyone around him better, he also was a free spirit from whom I learned much. His questions encouraged me to explain myself in ways I had never done before. And his willingness to listen to my answers, to accept those answers—even if he wasn't convinced—is the foundation of a relationship I enjoy so much today. Bill makes it a point to share breakfast with me regularly . . . and I look forward to every one of those meals!

—John Wooden

. . . .

JOHN WOODEN WAS MY HERO long before I ever met him.

I started playing basketball in 1960, when I was eight years old and loved playing by myself. Basketball was the perfect game for me because I stuttered so severely whenever I tried to speak. You could play by yourself and didn't have to talk to anyone. It's really the only team sport you can practice by yourself and have any fun at all.

When I wasn't playing basketball, I was listening to it. I had a small, handheld transistor radio, and from our home in San Diego I would listen to Chick Hearn on the Laker games and the UCLA Bruin broadcasts. The way he described basketball taught me how to think about the game, how to visualize it, how to dream it, how to love and live it.

The first time I saw basketball played on TV was when, at a friend's house, I got to watch Gail Goodrich's championship game performance in 1965. From that moment, I knew what I wanted to do with the rest of my life. I was a small, skinny, scrawny child at a time when the UCLA teams were led by Goodrich, Keith Erickson, Kenny Washington, Walt Hazzard— all the little fast guys who to this day are still my favorite players. With John Wooden as their coach, they played the game with precision, passion, and as a team. They needed each other to be successful. That's what I enjoyed about basketball then and what still drives my love for the game today.

And no one could make a team come together like Coach Wooden.

SHORTLY AFTER I first started to play ball, Coach Wooden came to San Diego to put on a basketball clinic. My first basketball coach, Rocky, somehow scraped together the entrance fee so I could go. As I sat there listening to this master teacher I'd heard on the radio and read so much about in the newspapers, I was mesmerized by his simple, direct, and enthusiastic approach. He spoke about footwork, balance, and the team. He ran us through drills and mental exercises all based on his Pyramid of Success. At about the same time as I went to the clinic, the championship streak at UCLA was beginning. Then a few years later, Kareem came to UCLA and he was everybody's hero, the most incredible player ever. That made everything even better for a young boy from San Diego with huge dreams.

During my senior year at Helix High School, I was offered the chance to play at UCLA as well. Other schools didn't need to waste their time in the recruiting game. I knew from the outset where I wanted to go, what I wanted to do—and who I wanted to learn from. Every coach I ever had was a huge John Wooden disciple, so the team game—the fast break, the pressure defense, the passing, the fundamentals—was what I was taught from the beginning. I had dreamed for years of playing for John Wooden. During my four years at UCLA, I discovered that the reality was even better than I could have ever imagined.

I ARRIVED AT UCLA as a freshman in 1970 and couldn't wait to get to the first practice. As much as I loved studying in the library, going to church, riding my bike, and playing beach volleyball, the anticipation of being in the same gym with John Wooden was almost more than I could stand.

We were all warming up at Pauley Pavilion with palpable excitement when Coach Wooden came out that first day, this little old guy—he was sixty-one and we were mere teenagers, many of us barely seventeen years old. Coach said, "Okay, you new guys come with me." I figured he was going to let us play on the side court by ourselves to see who had a game. Instead, he took us back into the locker room. We thought maybe he was going to share some secret knowledge—give us the keys to what it took to become a great UCLA champion.

I was there with the other freshmen in what was considered a pretty dynamic recruiting class—Jamal Wilkes, Greg Lee, Hank Babcock, Vince Carson, and Gary Franklin. When we were all settled, Coach said, "Pay attention. This is how you put on your shoes and socks." We all looked at each other in disbelief.

Then he took off his own shoes and socks, and you could see his varicose veins and hammertoes. Meticulously, he demonstrated how to put our socks on so they wouldn't wrinkle, pulling them over our toes, around the heel, and up at the ankle, smoothing them out from the bottom up along the way. He took the same approach with his shoes, tightening the laces from bottom to top until the shoe fit snuggly before double-tying them so they would not come undone. He made the point that it was critically important that our equipment was always in perfect order and condition, and never to allow things under our control to fail.

When the lecture ended, we all looked at each other in bewilderment. Did that really just happen? Did the smartest man in college basketball really just teach us how to smooth our socks? It seemed ridiculous.

Then Coach looked at us and made the point: "If your socks and shoes aren't properly fitted, your foot will slide in your shoe during practice. That will lead to blisters. If you have blisters, you won't practice. If you don't practice, you won't play. If you're not in the game, it's tough to be successful." He finished with "Okay, let's go!" Then he turned and walked back out to the court. We dutifully followed and have been doing so ever since.

As time passed I came to realize that his inaugural lesson— one he began teaching when he was a high school coach in Indiana and had seen many players develop blisters—was among the greatest gifts Coach Wooden ever gave me: the importance of basic lessons and skills. That day he was giving us something to build on—a foundation. He really was giving us the keys to a kingdom. The lesson was simple: You can only be successful at the big things if you do the little things right. Or put another way: If you don't have time to do it right the first time, when will you ever find the time to do it over?

Through years of observing him and his meticulous attention to detail, I realized that his teaching was timeless, like a Grateful Dead, Bob Dylan, or Neil Young song. Everything went back to the foundation—the building blocks, the structure upon which success is built. I have followed this and many of his other lessons ever since. I even tie my dress shoes the same way today!

Our family home is now a shrine to John Wooden. Pictures, pyramids, stories, event memorabilia and letters are all over the place. As I sit here at my desk I am surrounded by pictures of Coach peering at me from every angle, and I can hear him saying, "What are you doing, Walton? And why aren't you getting more done? Goodness gracious sakes alive, how many times do I have to tell you—never mistake activity for achievement!"

Coach wrote me a short congratulatory note when I won the NBA's Sixth Man of the Year Award in 1986 with the Celtics—which basically confirmed that I was Larry Bird's valet. The note said, "Congratulations. You have finally figured out two of life's most important lessons. You have learned to be quick without hurrying and you have learned that failing to prepare is preparing to fail." I have that framed here at the house, and I walk by it every day. Funny, I have no idea where the award is, but I have the letter framed.

NOT SURPRISINGLY, OUR children grew up under the Wooden umbrella. As our four boys were coming into their own, I had matured enough to realize that I had not taken full advantage of Coach's brilliance while at UCLA. Those missed opportunities remain a great regret, but I tried to make up for this by passing those lessons on to my sons. During my NBA days, I was injured a lot and regularly traveled from our home in San Diego to Los Angeles to see the doctors. I would try to take the boys with me so they could get to know Coach. We would go over to his house, and like most parents of young children visiting their elders, I was always getting them to pull their pants up, turn their hats around, and tie their shoes. They had no idea at the time—just as I had not—how special and rare an opportunity this was.

As each of the boys—Adam, Nathan, Luke, and Chris—got older, I asked Coach to teach them how to put on their socks and shoes! Ever the teacher and always willing to work, Coach reprised the first encounter I had with him: "These laces aren't right. You've got a wrinkle here, this heel is not lined up properly. This shoe doesn't fit correctly. What is your father doing? Didn't he learn anything while under my supervision?"

While Coach was working with each son, I tried to chime in. They would give me that look of "Dad—shut up"—the same look I used to give Coach years ago. He would be on the sideline barking his endless maxims—"Be quick, but don't hurry . . . Failing to prepare is preparing to fail . . . Never mistake activity for achievement . . . The worst things you can do for the ones you love are the things they could and should do for themselves"—and I would mumble, "Shut up, Coach, just let us play. It's our game. Let us be." Thankfully, he never heard me.

Years later, as our children chased down their dreams—each went on to play NCAA basketball, Adam at LSU, Nathan at Princeton, Luke at Arizona State, and Chris at San Diego State—I would find myself constantly repeating the mantras: "Be quick, but don't hurry. Failing to prepare is preparing to fail. Never mistake activity for achievement. Happiness begins when self-ishness ends." I had even written Coach's maxims on their lunch bags every day. They were always so embarrassed.

As I tried to pass those great lessons along to my sons, I could see and feel Coach standing ever so quietly in the background with his arms folded gently across his chest, shaking his head in dismay and disappointment, and saying, "Walton, you are indeed the slowest learner I've ever had."

PEOPLE ARE OFTEN confused and disappointed when they see video of Coach Wooden on the sideline during a game. He just sat there in his chair—never drawing attention to himself, his program rolled up, observing everything, life unfolding before him according to plan. His reasoning was simple: His work was done on the practice floor. In practice, he was the algebra, history, or music teacher, and when he gave an exam—for us it was the games—there was no further instruction offered, allowed, or necessary. It was up to us, his students, to get things done, and he made that very clear every day. It was our world, our game—meant to be played a certain way.

Despite being stern and demanding, yet always fair, Coach constantly made it so much fun to practice, play, and be a part of his special team. It was a glorious celebration and privilege to go to his practices—his classroom, his laboratory—every day.

Even though his drills were always the same, and most often their order as well, they were mentally stimulating. He had invented all of them over many years. At the beginning there was no ball involved in the drills. If you only do the drill with a ball, you focus on the result (i.e., Did you make the shot?), not on building the fundamental base. How do you land? Do you come down in proper balance, always ready for what is next? Nobody was ever late for practice. Nobody wanted it to end.

When any of us reflects on what he taught us, it always comes down to learning how to learn and how to compete. With those two qualities, you can do anything you want. He taught us how to build a life and a world for the rest of our days. To him it was never really basketball, it was life itself.

Players who never get that kind of exposure have no idea what is missing in their game and life. They think practice is about strategy and a coach trying to tell them what to do in an infinite galaxy of situations. Nothing could be farther from the truth. Practice is skill development, physical fitness, and a chance to develop and refine the decision-making processes on the court. The game is too fast for that responsibility to rest anywhere else. You train yourself how to make the correct decisions, and that's where Coach Wooden was at his best. He sought out pupils who had an insatiable lust for knowledge and success, and taught them his four laws of learning: demonstration, imitation, correction, and repetition. It sounds easy, but it is extremely hard work, and you have to have the right leader who is able to show you the way. You have to listen and be corrected properly. You have to endlessly repeat everything. Ultimately you get it—and become the teacher yourself as the circle becomes complete.

COACH AND I disagreed about many things away from the game, and I never hesitated to remind him of those differences. But he always had the last word.

There's a famous story about photo day of my senior year when I showed up with a beard and long hair. Coach had rules against each, but I felt that his rules were outdated, and I chose to challenge him on this one. When I explained my reasoning, Coach gave me a look that was more sympathetic than stern. Then he said, "Bill, I acknowledge that you have a right to disagree with my rules. But I'm the coach here, and we're sure going to miss you."

Coach then walked away. I had been MVP of two straight championship teams. Would he really dismiss me over a silly rule? I wasn't about to find out. I grabbed a bicycle and raced to the nearest barbershop and got my hair cut and beard shaved. I was back in what seemed like fifteen minutes.

Years later, we discussed whether he would really have dismissed me over the length of my hair. Showing once again how timeless his wisdom was, Coach said simply and with a sly grin, "All that matters, Bill, is that at that moment you believed that I would."

FROM THE OUTSIDE, all of Coach's maxims and teachings of the fundamentals of life appear simple, obvious, and (to some people) even silly. But life teaches us that they only seem this way when things are going well in one's life. When the ball bounces the other way and things have crumbled around you and you have to get back up to start over one more time—then you discover how hard and complex those lessons can be.

During the toughest challenges in my life I've come to most appreciate all Coach Wooden means to me. The things he would say—"Don't lie, don't cheat, don't steal, don't whine, don't complain, don't make excuses; worry about the things you can control, and not the things you can't"—were endless. Yet there is an appropriate one for every situation. The real challenge is to find the one that fits and try to make it work for you.

When I left UCLA and joined the NBA, it was the first time in my life that basketball was not about the team. It was about individual agendas, selfishness, greed, and money—the antitheses of what John Wooden stood for. All the things I lived for in basketball now came into question. When, after fourteen years, my pro career came to a crashing halt, the result of an endless string of injuries, I found myself really up against things, as I could barely walk, much less play the game of my dreams anymore. Over time, all the things Coach had offered me over so many years became ever more important to me. As I said, he taught me how to learn, how to live. Now the stutterer who showed up at UCLA is a television broadcaster.

I was so sad when Coach retired because I thought he would lose the necessary platform that allowed him to change the lives of others. Instead, the opposite has occurred. As he has aged, his self-built stage is today so much grander than it ever was. What a testament to the enduring value, breadth, and depth of his message. In the early years he was teaching twelve young student-athletes in the afternoon. Now his students are often business leaders, writers, and those who have studied Coach's philosophies—and his classroom never ends. Indeed, I believe he and his system could be just as successful if he were still on the sideline, and the reason is simple: His philosophies would still attract the very best to his campus.

Consider, for example, how much fun and success the 2008 U.S. Olympic basketball team—entirely made up of NBA stars— had in Beijing with the structure and organization that Duke coach Mike Krzyzewski and Jerry Colangelo provided. Their discipline in practice, their preparation—ensuring there was no wasted time, no wasted energy, no standing around, no coaches giving long speeches—was a modern-day version of Coach Wooden's practice plan.

Today, through his speeches and correspondence, appearances, video conferences, and book projects such as this one, through his mere existence, John Wooden directly impacts the lives of many, many thousands of people. Thanks, Coach, for being a beacon of hope and inspiration, for being our shining star and moral compass. We extend our eternal gratitude for your gifts of life and more so for your everlasting patience.

And just as you closed so many of your lesson plans to us over the years, it is fitting to remind everyone one last time that through this book *you* have done your job; the rest is now up to us.

CHAPTER 12

Andy Hill

When people ask me about coaching players at UCLA, the conversation routinely starts with Bill Walton and Lewis Alcindor. But while there were a few All-Americans on our teams, there was a much greater number of players who weren't as well known. Many of those players were stars at the high school level, but for whatever reason found themselves falling into role player positions in college. I have often said that while your star may be your engine, your role players provide the wheels, and an engine is obviously no good without wheels. Andy Hill was a wheel. Some of those players willingly took to that role. Others weren't so willing—and Andy was one of those. He loved to question decisions and challenge authority. When he left UCLA, he did so as a champion, but not a happy one. It took years for us to finally reach the point where we could discuss his years at UCLA, but when we did, it changed the relationship forever. I have learned a lot about mentoring— including ways I wished I had reached him years ago—from many years of breakfasts with Andy.

—John Wooden

· · · · · · · ·

IN THE THREE DECADES THAT HAVE passed since my basketball-playing days at UCLA, the golf course has become a great outlet for my competitiveness. By its nature, golf is a humbling game; it can bring the best of players down. At the same time, it can be incredibly uplifting. So it's fitting that the golf course was where I came upon a revelation that changed my life.

One day, while I was wrestling with an erratic swing, my playing partner offered a simple suggestion: "You're hurrying; slow down and get your balance." Those words sounded eerily familiar. I realized in a moment that they were almost identical to the instruction my UCLA basketball teammates and I had received regularly from Coach John Wooden: "Be quick—but don't hurry," he would tell us. "Balance is everything."

Though I had heard that advice more times in my life than I could count, my partner's simple advice on the golf course that day broke down a twenty-five-year-old wall between me and a man who had inspired me more than I knew.

I HAD GROWN up playing basketball in Southern California, and every time I took the ball out on the court, even just to shoot free throws, I was fantasizing about a starring role on my hometown Bruins, then a national powerhouse. I enrolled at UCLA after earning All-City honors at University High in nearby West Los Angeles. One newspaper article described me as a "right-handed Gail Goodrich," referring to the sharp-shooting All-American Bruins guard I had idolized as a youngster. On the UCLA freshman team, already confident in my abilities, I shared MVP honors with future All-American Henry Bibby. It seemed only natural that I would make a sim-

ilar ascent: I'd join the varsity as a sophomore and help continue the string of championships Coach's teams were then
extending.

If only it had turned out that way. Over the next three seasons,
I was relegated to riding the bench as we won three consecutive
National Championships. I had philosophical differences with
Coach and his teaching style—which I unabashedly shared
with him—and I couldn't help but think that my lack of playing
time had more to do with my outspokenness than with my ability on the court. I finished my last year having hardly played at
all, feeling like I'd never even had the chance to prove myself—
never gotten to be the player I was in my mind. By the time
graduation arrived, I was just glad that my time on the team
was over. I had made myself miserable, and I was so sure that
Coach Wooden had kept me from my dream that when I graduated, I decided to sever ties with the program I had long loved
and the man I held in such high regard.

I went on to play basketball in Israel, coached at a community college, ran a research center, and eventually made my way
to a career in show business. John Wooden was way back in my
rearview mirror. Nevertheless, that hurt always lingered. I remember, many years after graduating, playing a round of golf
with a business acquaintance and a longtime Bruin fan who remembered me from those championship teams. He had introduced me to the other members of our foursome that day as
the man whose mere presence could start five thousand cars—
because when I got into the game, everyone in the crowd was
leaving. I laughed at the joke, but inside the pain was still there.

So here I was, once again on the golf course, confronted by
my past. Only this time, the words of advice from my playing
partner stirred an entirely different response. "Be quick—but
don't hurry." As much as I wanted to forget those days, Coach
Wooden's words were so clearly ingrained in my memory.

Though I never intended to call Coach again, I knew that's what I had to do. Everything I had learned to ensure success in my life—from raising a family to achieving the presidency of CBS Productions—had been taught to me by Coach Wooden. I was *raised* to be a Wooden mentee. My high school basketball coach was Courtney Borio, who had played at UCLA. And I was on UCLA's freshman team under the instruction of Gary Cunningham, who also was one of Coach's former students. So by the time I walked into Coach Wooden's huddle, I had spent four years learning from those who had learned from him.

Were it not for my scholarship to UCLA, I would have missed out on the opportunity of being mentored by the greatest coach in college basketball history. But it took me twenty-five years to understand two of the great truisms of mentoring: You often don't recognize your mentors at the time they're deeply involved in your life; and mentoring often occurs even when you don't want it to. How many times have we all been blind to how much we learned from our parents—or how much they knew about life—until years after leaving home? Such was the case between Coach Wooden and me.

IT TOOK ME some time to find the nerve to reconnect, and when I did, the only contact I had for him was the old telephone number he had given his players decades ago. Without much confidence, I took a deep breath and dialed. Coach picked up. The number hadn't changed, and whether by fate or mere good fortune, he was sitting by the phone when I made the call. It was one of the luckiest breaks of my life.

Reuniting with him after a quarter century proved cathartic. Instead of holding Coach Wooden responsible for my shortcomings on the basketball court, I realized that my days with the Bruins were the greatest experience a young man could have.

Even though it wasn't everything I wanted it to be, I had gotten a lot out of it. And over time, I actually grew to understand that this was true because I *didn't* play. Having to sit on the bench taught me humility, which I didn't have much of when I started at UCLA. When I left school and went into the business world, I was hungry because I felt like I had been a failure. That gave me a drive I wouldn't have had if I had played as much as I wanted to.

Yet for all of that, I wanted Coach to be proud of me, and when we reconnected, he told me that some of the shows I was involved with were some of his favorites—*Touched by an Angel* and *Walker, Texas Ranger* were two he mentioned—and then I finally realized I *had* made him proud. It's funny, because I knew that Coach would like those shows. There's an element of this that's almost embarrassing because I had that great opportunity in college and I just refused to recognize it as such at the time. But by reconnecting with Coach, I closed that loop. When I left his apartment that first day, I pulled around the corner and cried. The weight I was carrying with me—the sense of disappointment, the frustration, all my feelings of failure—was gone.

ONE OF THE greatest lessons I learned from Coach is that winning isn't the way you measure success. That can be a difficult concept for a young person, especially if you happened to play for the Bruins, where winning sometimes seemed like a natural part of the game of basketball.

In my three varsity seasons at UCLA, we compiled an 87–3 record and won three National Championships. The seeds of that success were sown on the practice court. This was Coach Wooden's classroom, and despite my disappointment in games, it was the one place I looked forward to being every day. While the daily practices provided me with a chance to show my abilities as a player, they were unknowingly cementing the life skills

I would carry forward well beyond my days with the Bruins. I learned many of life's great lessons in the practice gym—and while sitting on the bench. And they had soaked in, no matter how hardheaded I had been.

My son, Aaron, is an extraordinary musician, an oboist. After earning an undergraduate degree from the University of Michigan's School of Music and a master's from Yale, he set out to find a job in an orchestra. The music world is really tough, in many ways as competitive as the world of sports; you don't always get what you want. Aaron is very talented, but in audition after audition, even though he did well, he felt the disappointment of being rejected.

Several years ago Aaron was taking part in the Henry Mancini Institute at UCLA, which put ninety kids from around the world in a four-week program to give them a taste of what it's like to play in a Hollywood soundstage orchestra, allowing them to interface with some of the finest musicians in the world. On the first day of camp he was in competition with a twenty-three-year-old named Tom Owen, who is among the best young oboists in the world. Auditions were held to play solos the last night, a gala affair that every big name in the music industry attends. The night of the audition, I called Aaron and asked how his solo had gone.

"I did great!" he said. I was ecstatic. "Oh, great!" I said. "You won?"

"No, but I played really well," he said, clearly happy. "I was prepared, and that's all I can control. The other guy, Tom, he was really good, Dad. But I did the best that I could, and I'm happy with that."

"Good for you," I said, awestruck. "There's no stopping you now."

You could have caught flies in my mouth. He was twenty years old, and he understood what success really was. Because of the way I felt about Coach Wooden, Aaron hadn't been as exposed to him as he might have been—and to the degree that he was, he had heard my frustrations with Coach. But despite this, the leadership ideas about what's important that Coach instilled in me were passed on to him.

Over the course of the camp Aaron and Tom became best buddies. At the end of the session, as they got ready to perform, Tom's oboe broke. Aaron was next in line to play. But rather than take Tom's spot, Aaron set out to help him get his oboe repaired. It took all day to find a repairman, because everyone serious in the local music scene was at an international convention in Canada. But Aaron kept on it, got Tom's oboe fixed, and then watched as his friend performed.

And just as Coach Wooden taught, that effort at being a great teammate paid off. At the end of the performance, Tom was offered an opportunity by a record producer to play on an album. Tom looked at the producer and said, "For what you're looking for, I would tell you Aaron Hill is a better fit." And Aaron got to play and get the recording credit.

Today Tom is with a major symphony in Cologne, Germany. My son has become a John Wooden–like oboe teacher, working as a professor at the University of Virginia. The two are still good friends.

WHAT IS REALLY heartwarming to me is the relationship that Aaron has struck up with Coach over the past few years. Whenever he comes into town he wants to have breakfast with him. The bond between my son, an accomplished musician, and Coach is an interesting one. Getting a group of people to create together is what basketball—and music—are about. You've got to have a structure, but you also need to leave space for creativity within structure, and really talented, creative people are the hardest to blend into a unit. But if you can do that, which Coach was able to over time, you've got something special.

In the first days of January 2009, Aaron was home, and I took him to breakfast with Coach. Aaron jokingly said, "So how is 2009 treating you so far?" It was just a throwaway line, but Coach looked at him seriously and said, "No complaints—but you'll probably get that same answer if you ask me again on December thirty-first."

What a great lesson. Don't complain. Keep your head down. Keep doing the right thing. We now have breakfast together regularly, and every time I leave one of those breakfasts, I pinch myself that I'm still learning—and that he's still teaching.

I NEVER HAD the opportunity to realize my dreams on the court with the Bruins; the same dreams held by former teammates such as Bill Walton, Henry Bibby, and Sidney Wicks, who continued to live theirs postgraduation with NBA careers. That didn't prevent me from telling my story on a different professional stage. After learning the television business at a small company and then supervising movies and miniseries for Columbia Television, I formed my own production company. My first project was a family movie shot on location in Ireland.

Three Wishes for Jamie told the story of a young Irish lad who was granted three wishes by a magical queen: the chance to travel, to marry the girl of his dreams, and to father a son who spoke Gaelic. Jamie realized his first two dreams, but when his wife was unable to conceive, he felt his last wish had escaped him. They chose to adopt a son. Sadly, the boy was mute.

Depressed, Jamie's life began to unravel, until the dramatic final scene, when the boy finally speaks. At that point, Jamie realized that all three of his wishes had been granted.

Not until the movie's rough-cut screening, well over a year into the process, did I realize that the story wasn't solely about an Irish kid with wild dreams. It was about me. Growing up in Westwood, I had fantasized about the improbable chance to play for Coach Wooden's fabled Bruins. That opportunity became a reality, and over the course of my career UCLA won three NCAA championships. Yet I was unhappy due to my lack of playing time. Like my life, the movie had certain wishes at the heart of its plot. But mine had to do with things left unresolved.

FROM MY EARLIEST days as a fan, and later as a Bruin recruit, I viewed Coach Wooden as a very simple, almost Zen-like character. With his midwestern roots and the sweet wholesomeness of the man in the Pepperidge Farm commercials, he seemed above it all. He was a low-pressure recruiter who sold prospects on the opportunity to attend a great university and play for a fine staff. Add into the mix the fact that the Bruins played fast and that they won—a lot—and who wouldn't want to play at UCLA? When I was being recruited, Coach seemed like a combination of the best attributes of my dad and my granddad.

I had a much more difficult time seeing those softer qualities during my four years on campus. I recognized soon after my arrival that Coach could be really tough and stubborn. Though he always told us his office door was open, and I had many visits to Coach's office, nothing good came of any of them. These were very difficult times. Student activism was running at an all-time high, especially among the majority who denounced the ongoing Vietnam War, and we were influenced by the peace marches and the various forms of freedom of speech and expression.

I quickly made the wrong impression on Coach. I approached him in his office on the eve of my first UCLA practice with the idea that he should postpone the first workout so that my teammates and I could participate in a protest of the war. Coach was fine with us going to the protest, but practice would not be canceled. The way he said it let me know that I had better be there.

Through the years there would be other encounters between the two of us, over things as simple as his haircut policy—he didn't allow anyone with long hair to play on his team—or as involved as the letter we sent to President Richard Nixon on behalf of the "National Champion" UCLA basketball team, denouncing the Vietnam War. My belief that Coach was "socially unjust" was made worse, I'm sure, by my unhappiness over playing time with the varsity. I was convinced there was a direct correlation between my political activism and outspoken nature and the number—the very small number—of minutes I was logging during games.

Coach Wooden was conditionally flexible, I would say. However, in his core beliefs—about being on time, not swearing, keeping your hair cut—he wasn't flexible at all. Back then, I thought the rule about hair was the dumbest thing I had ever heard. In retrospect, it was really smart because by enforcing a rule that everybody thought was dumb, Coach ultimately impressed on us that he was the only person in charge. Looking back at the personalities and egos with which he was contending (and mine was one of the most difficult), I now understand why this was essential. Eventually I came to realize that the prevailing sentiment of the 1960s and '70s—that everyone should be treated the same everywhere, all the time—was in fact not true in the real world.

I remember being significantly late for a team dinner while

goofing off with All-American center Bill Walton. Upon our tardy arrival in the hotel dining room, only two seats remained open. Bill moved faster than I and took the empty seat at the far end of the table . . . and I was stuck next to Coach. Sheepishly, we sat down, fully expecting to feel Coach's wrath. As it turned out, neither of us got disciplined.

Had I been running late with some of my fellow scrubs, we probably would have been in trouble, but it would have had more to do with our perceived disrespect than anything else. Coach really seemed to understand people's attitudes. If my tardiness seemed to be the result of me just not caring, or trying to make some point of defiance, I would have merited a dressing down. But because I happened to be with someone who genuinely cared and was always open to instruction, correction, and the way things were run, Coach probably recognized our lateness as a genuine accident. Coach Wooden didn't treat everybody the same; he treated people the way they deserved to be treated.

Years later, I was overseeing the production of the television series *Dr. Quinn, Medicine Woman,* starring the actress Jane Seymour. On the first day that we went into production, I got a call from the set that Jane didn't want to come out of her trailer. She had learned that the network management had such little faith in the show that they intended to pull if off the fall schedule.

Despite her impressive prior film career, this was Jane's first television series, and the crazy world of ratings rumors was new to her. She was crushed and wondered why she should do episodes of a series that was not going to continue.

As head of production for CBS, I usually handled these types of problems on the telephone. But this was Jane Seymour, so I drove out from my Beverly Hills office. I went into Jane's trailer and explained to her that she had to come out of the trailer, and after a short discussion, she did. Jane is not just a star, she is also a friend, and there would be no show without her. She had earned and deserved the star treatment.

UCLA HAS OCCASIONAL industry nights when they bring in graduates who have been successful in various fields to offer students advice. Sometime in the late 1980s, before Coach and I had reconnected, UCLA held an entertainment industry night. A young woman called me in advance to ask a few questions for the alumni magazine, among them what class I learned the most from at UCLA. Sometimes you spit things out unfiltered, and this was one of those moments. "Coach Wooden's class," I said. "But he didn't teach a class," she responded. "He sure did," I said. "From three to five-thirty P.M. Monday through Friday. Trust me."

Verbalizing this started the process that led to my moment of epiphany on the golf course, and to my realization that Coach Wooden's impact on my life was far more pervasive than I had realized. I had adopted his values, his system of leadership, and had done so unwittingly.

All the things I learned in those classes—not to quit, to commit myself to something bigger than myself, to finish everything, to understand that peace of mind is the true meaning of success—have benefited me in the course of my career. Now that I have passed those lessons to my son, and he passes them to his students, I know that the true power of Coach's mentorship is the unbroken chain between him, his "boys," and their children. That is a true mentor's great legacy.

CHAPTER 13

Roy Williams

I still watch college basketball when I can and attend as many UCLA home games as possible. Until I turned ninety, I would try to get out to see practice at some schools— that's the part of the game I really miss. Mike Krzyzewski invited me to observe a practice at Duke a few years ago; he even invited me to conduct the practice, an offer I politely declined. The precision with which Duke runs its practice, the minute-to-minute management of the entire period, brought back great memories. But in recent years, as I've eliminated most all of my air travel, I stopped going to the Final Four or the coaching conventions. As a result, my interaction with many of today's coaches has been limited to answering my home phone when one of them might call or welcoming them to my home if one might choose to visit. It surprises many people when they find out that of the coaches who choose to stop in, more women's college coaches and high school coaches have done so than coaches from the men's college game. One of the few who has kept me on his call and visit list has been Roy Williams, the coach at North Carolina who won a

great National Championship in 2009 with as talented a
group of players as I've seen in a while. What impressed
me so was how Coach Williams kept all of that talent
playing together as a team, one that was well disciplined
and fundamentally sound. That is the result of the way he
teaches his players and the way they respect him. Coach
Williams has been to my home a few times, and the more
I've come to know him the more convinced I am that he is
the kind of coach I would have enjoyed working with and
learning from.

—John Wooden

. . . .

I HAVE TO ADMIT THAT I WAS A LITTLE surprised when I learned
that Coach Wooden thought of me as he was building a book
on mentoring. It might be better said that I was surprised Coach
Wooden thought of me at all. There's no question that I would
list him among the most influential men in my basketball life,
dating back to a clinic I attended more than thirty years ago.
For most of my career, his importance has had little to do with
personal interaction; I only knew him from afar. But he's always
been, since my days as a high school coach, someone I looked
up to. I can remember, during my first year in high school
coaching in 1973–74, driving from Asheville, North Carolina, to
Jacksonville, Florida, to hear him speak at a coaches' clinic. I
did the same a year later, driving to another clinic, in Greens-
boro, North Carolina.

What I'll always remember about those talks is not what
he shared about his many wins and a few losses but the way he
conducted himself, the way he served as a role model to those
of us who hoped to be as successful as he was in our profession.
And I'll remember getting a copy of his Pyramid of Success,

which has been hanging on the wall of my office for years. I enjoy looking at each block and piecing it together. I'm big on enthusiasm and industriousness, and I try to practice them regularly.

But the greatest lesson Coach Wooden has taught me has nothing to do with basketball, and it has been learned later in my career. About ten years ago, while I was still the coach at Kansas, I saw him at the Final Four and he said something he had said to me two or three times previously: "Roy, sometime when you're in Los Angeles, why don't you give me a call and come on by and see me." When he said it that time, for some reason I realized what an idiot I had been to waste such wonderful prior opportunities. As I think about it now, I guess the reason I didn't respond the first couple of times he made the offer was that I figured he was just being polite, and also I was a little in awe and uncertain of what he could possibly want to talk to me about. It finally clicked that this legend in our game was truly extending an opportunity for me to come and learn from him.

The next time I knew I was headed to the West Coast, I have to admit I was still a little unsure, so I called his daughter Nan to set it up. I confessed to her that I had done so because I still felt like it would be a bother to Coach if I called him directly and, frankly, she seemed easier to bother. She laughed and understood what I meant, let me know I was worrying more than I should, and set up the meeting.

I went by on a Sunday afternoon and spent a couple of hours with him. By the end of that time I was thinking that at nearly ninety years old, Coach must be getting tired. I said, "Coach, why don't I get out of your hair?" He said, "No, don't rush. Have you eaten?" I was a little surprised, but at his suggestion we went out to dinner down the street, spent another couple of hours talking, and then we came back to his house. By that time

I had been with him almost five hours and loved every minute of it. He invited me back in and we talked some more. It was as if he had more energy than nearly anyone I knew.

He also had a memory—for both things in the past and things happening today—that blew me away. During that day together, he told me a Gail Goodrich recruiting story from 1961 or 1962, then he told me about one of the games he had watched my team play that year with great detail, and he then gave me a full recap of what had gone on that day at the Masters because I had left to go see him at about four, and the Masters was over by then. I sat there amazed at how precise his memory was.

If it was possible, my admiration grew for him that day. And I walked away with an enormous lesson. Here was an opportunity to be mentored by one of the greatest coaches of all time, and I didn't take it until he made the offer repeatedly. I don't know why I didn't, but I'll never miss an opportunity like that again. When those of us who are learning are given those chances, it is our responsibility to take advantage of them. And when I make an offer for a younger coach to come visit, I make sure they know I hope they take me up on the offer.

One thing about my time with Coach: I always learn something that surprises me. I try to come prepared with some questions, looking for some perspective. But I usually end up with a little something I wasn't planning for. Like the time he told me that before every season when he was at UCLA he would take out a sheet of paper, make his way through the schedule, and predict the team's final record. He would put the paper in an envelope and in his desk drawer. It was interesting because he told me he never predicted his team would go undefeated— though they did four times—and that the exercise allowed him to think through the year and plan accordingly. It helped him build practice plans, and he made sure to build momentum at key points in the year. I was surprised he would do anything like that.

With the door open, I found myself looking for opportunities to talk to Coach. A couple of those conversations occurred around two of the toughest decisions I've had to make professionally—when the North Carolina head coaching job opened up in 2000 and again in 2003. On both occasions I was as happy as I could imagine at Kansas, but I was torn by the opportunity to return to my alma mater. Because of all he had accomplished, I certainly valued Coach's perspective. In 2000 when we were together, I asked him why he never went back to his alma mater, Purdue. I knew at the time that it wouldn't be long before I would be asked that question about coming back to North Carolina, and I was wondering if he had ever considered going home while working at a job he definitely enjoyed.

He told me "If you"—and he stressed the *you*—"think about it, you'll make the right decision. Go home and ask the question— ask your wife and your family—and there you will find the answer." It was great and very subtly delivered advice. He was telling me who to listen to . . . and who not to listen to. Don't let boosters or other people put pressure on you. Do what's right for your family and you'll never be unhappy. It was great advice because he knew that what my family wanted would be important to me, not what a bunch of people wanted me to do or wanted me not to do. That year, I stayed at Kansas, though in 2003 I knew the time was right, and I made the move to North Carolina.

In the years since that first visit, I've taken more time to both keep in touch with Coach and to talk to those who played for and coached with him over the years. Go past all the championships, all the wins, and when you realize what he means to all his former players, that gets right to the heart of mentoring. The more I learn about those relationships, the more I see why he is such an example for other coaches. I've learned just as much by listening to the way he talks about his players as I have by listening to what his players say about him. When you see players hold him in such reverence, when you see the way they so respect him, that tells you he did much more than just coach them. And when you listen to him talk about those players, you see what he learned from them.

Clearly a lot of his players see Coach Wooden as a father figure. That's an interesting place to be as a coach. For my part, I always try to make sure my players know that their father and mother come first and must be their biggest role models. I always say when I recruit players that I am not there to take the place of parents, but I will try to be a bridge between home and college when they come to me as a freshman . . . and then by the time they leave, they should no longer need a bridge. I know that's what Coach Wooden felt, too.

Coach Wooden's interest in and kindness to me as we developed our relationship led me to attend a number of events just to honor him and for an opportunity to spend time around him. I would go to certain banquets because I knew he would be there . . . and I even stopped going to one because I had learned that they hadn't treated him well. That's how much I respect him. What amazed me was that every time I saw him, he asked about something happening with my team or in my life that he clearly had followed. He always joked that in retirement he had time to keep track of his friends.

Interestingly, I was invoking Coach's name and what I perceived was his relationship with players long before that first sit-down at his home. When I was hired at Kansas in 1988 by Bob Frederick, I told him, "If you want someone to just coach, I'm not the guy. If you want someone to run a program like Dean Smith and John Wooden, that would be the job I would love to have." With Coach Wooden, it wasn't so much about basketball, it was about life. It wasn't, "This is what we're going to do against the zone defense." Rather, it was, "This is how we're going to carry ourselves as men, win or lose." That's what I told Bob Frederick I wanted to be like as a coach when I went to Kansas. And that's exactly what Kansas was looking for.

Though I hadn't spent much time around him then, I felt like I knew the kind of person Coach Wooden had been because I played for and coached with a man who was much like him, Dean Smith, with whom I was an assistant for ten years. He is my most important mentor and has obviously had the greatest influence on me because I've been so much closer to him, but my relationship with Coach Wooden has been, even from a distance, unique for me.

His mentorship of me in the past ten years hasn't come solely through conversation. I read anything that is written about Coach Wooden, and from those stories or books, I learn. If I get a chance to meet with any of his former players, I ask questions and listen to stories. I go to Michael Jordan's camp every year in Las Vegas, and Bill Walton is sometimes there. I always ask Bill to tell me stories about Coach and to share with me how he's doing at that time. I try to keep in touch with his life without needing to call him. Over time I have come to feel very close to Coach, and I'm flattered that he would say the same about me. What I've learned is that when your affection is genuine, you don't have to call that person every day to remain close. True relationships, ones like you'll have with a mentor, remain strong through time and distance.

Just don't make the mistake I almost made and miss an opportunity to learn from someone special.

CHAPTER 14
· · · · · · · · · · · ·
Dale Brown

When our UCLA teams played a scrappy Utah State team in the 1968 NCAA Tournament West Regional, I remember hearing about a young Aggies assistant who was full of energy and recruiting several of the same players we wanted. He was never intimidated. And he didn't engage in the negative recruiting tactics that were a part of the game then and are an even greater part of the game now. That assistant, Dale Brown, went on to Washington State, where we played his team twice in the conference during the 1971–72 season. One year later, he accepted a head coaching job at Louisiana State University, a program that had been down for some time. I was surprised when, during the summer before his first season, Dale called my office at UCLA. He asked if I would be willing to let him tag along for a day or two and ask questions. I certainly didn't mind, because sharing knowledge is, after all, what we as teachers must do. I didn't expect what happened when he arrived.

—John Wooden

· · · · · · · ·

THE MOMENT I WAS HIRED AT LSU in 1972, I knew that I needed to reach out to the best people I could, in all walks of life—from the worlds of entertainment, public speaking, positive thinking, and, of course, basketball—for their advice. I wanted to ask questions about how they became successful and, more important, how they maintained their success.

Several people were on each list, but I thought I should start with those who had the greatest longevity in what they did. In entertainment I approached Lawrence Welk to ask him how a no-name guy from North Dakota rose to the top of his profession. I called Lawrence at his office in California, and he immediately invited me to visit. We became close friends, and I learned a great deal from him. In the speaking business I had studied Bob Richards for years, watching him on the old 16mm Wheaties films. He was the best I had ever heard. I went to his ranch in Gordon, Texas, where he allowed me to look through his library and to ask many questions.

In basketball, however, I had a list of one. If I wanted to learn, I needed to visit John Wooden. I knew, even as a young coach, that he wasn't the kind of man who showed off his knowledge; he just shared it naturally. As a result, people would seek him out. I decided to be one of them.

When I called Coach Wooden, he immediately invited me to spend five days with him. I knew I needed to prepare, so I decided to put a different letter of the alphabet on each page of a notepad and ask questions about words that began with that letter. John Wooden's answers were an invaluable education in basketball—and mentoring—in twenty-six letters. Here are a few examples:

ACHIEVEMENT. *What did he consider achievement?* The first thing he said was, "Don't ever mistake activity for achievement."

Then he added advice his father had given him: "Never try to be better than anyone else, but never cease to be the best you can be. That's achievement."

I talked to him about "attitude"—the attitude of players, coaches, his attitude toward the pressure of winning, and problems with players off the court. He told me that he always insisted on two things above all else in his players: That they were always trying to improve and always willing to put the team above themselves. If they weren't willing to do those things, he didn't want them at UCLA. Coach thought a moment, then added, "And if they don't have that attitude before they come, they probably aren't going to develop it once they get here."

BOX-AND-ONE DEFENSE. *Did he like it? What problems did it create for him when opponents ran it? And when they did, how did he attack it?* I quickly learned that he was not a believer in any kind of "gimmick defense." (However, the box-and-one was instrumental in their winning a National Championship one year when an assistant coach suggested they try it. So I guess that also goes to show that Coach knew how to adapt to circumstances.)

Then I asked him about bulletin boards: *Did he use them to motivate or instruct?* He said he used them mostly for announcements. Real motivation for him was more than placing a quote on a bulletin board, which he felt his players probably wouldn't look at anyway.

COACHES. *Whom did he admire, and why?* Press Maravich, my predecessor at LSU, was his immediate answer. They roomed together every year at a summer basketball camp at Campbell College, and Wooden said Press was the brightest basketball mind he ever encountered. He added that Press could swear up a blue streak, "but he could quote Scripture better than anyone I ever knew, too."

I then asked about correspondence: *Did he answer all of it, or did he have someone else do it?* As you might expect, Coach did his utmost to read—and answer—all correspondence himself, and I am testament to that truth. In fact, I keep a file in my desk to this day that is reserved solely for my correspondence from Coach, and at least three fourths of his letters are handwritten in his flawless penmanship. His personal touch impressed me that day and has impressed me ever since.

DEFENSIVE DRILLS. *What did he think were the best ones? And how long should you run them?* Coach's answer was simple: "You need to spend more time on offense than you ever do on defense because offense is the execution of five players at one time—and that involves far more precision."

EDUCATION. *Did he have study periods for the team? And how did he encourage his players to secure a college degree?* This was before the days of academic centers, which are now a staple of university athletic programs. Coach's answer, while no magic formula, was an effective philosophy: You did your work and you made the grades. It was the same lesson Piggy Lambert had instilled in him. You are at college to get a degree—so get your degree. In fact, Coach can rattle off the number of doctors and lawyers and preachers and business executives among his former players as quickly as he can rattle off his game statistics—and he's prouder of his players than his winning percentages.

FULL-COURT MAN-TO-MAN PRESS. *Did he run and jump, double-team, or stay man-to-man? And what were the drills he used?* It floored me to realize just how much he did without a basketball. Jump shots, pivots—his players went through all of the basic moves before he ever put a ball in their hands. I was reminded of a time when I was an assistant at Utah State and we were playing UCLA in the Regional Championship. They had the court for practice at one o'clock, and we had it at three. I sneaked in a little early to catch a glimpse of what Coach was doing with his team, and I can still see them going through the motions: dribble, stop, pivot, elbows out. "Come on!" Coach shouted to Curtis Rowe. "Get your elbows out!" Here it was the last practice before the big game and they were going over the fundamentals. Incredible but effective. They won that game against us.

HALFTIME ORGANIZATION. *When he addressed his team, what did he focus on first?* Coach probably dominated here more than anywhere else. He handled the locker room coolly and efficiently, explaining strategies and techniques to his players—and fielding questions. "No player ever asked as many questions as Bill Walton," he said with a laugh. "He always wanted to know the 'why' of things. When you have a player like that, do your best to answer as best you can. It's a great way to teach."

MOTIVATION. *How much did he do? How did he feel about motivational tactics?* He didn't use videos, he seldom brought in speakers. Coach's motivation was a wink and a tap on the leg, or walking by a guy and quietly saying, "Nice job, son." His players knew he wasn't a motivational guy in the traditional way, but I don't think he really had to pump up his players much, either. They were already excited to be playing (and winning) on his team.

THE FIRST DAY we started at eight A.M. By six P.M. we had been at it for ten hours, and I had started to feel that I was imposing on him. So I said, "Coach, I have taken enough of your time today and I'm sure you're tired. I'll see you tomorrow." He immediately fixed me with a look and said, "No, I'm not tired! Sit down and we'll continue." He went another four hours and never seemed to tire. I left at ten P.M. and came back the next day with fresh pages to fill in my notebook.

PHILOSOPHY. *What were his big-picture ideas on life, on discipline?* In both these areas, Coach again pointed me to the fundamentals. Focus on the basics. Work on passing drills in every possible way, and always do it at game pace, with and without defense. Do nothing else until your players execute them perfectly. He was saying things that every fifth grader in Indiana hears in gym class, such as, "Thumbs pointed down to the floor!" He impressed on me the importance of never letting my players lose sight of the fundamentals, or the rest of their game wouldn't be worth much. A foundation is the most solid part of a structure for a reason: It's the most important. A solid foundation sets the stage for everything else.

RECRUITING. *Was it true that he seldom went into a recruit's home?* Coach was well known for not actively recruiting, and I was fascinated to understand why. His answer gave me a telling insight into the success of his program: "If I feel like a young man is questioning if this is the right place, I don't want to talk him into coming," he reasoned. "I don't want anyone at UCLA who doesn't want to be here."

TIME-OUTS. *What was his philosophy?* Coach admitted that he never wanted to be the first one to call a time-out; he wanted to prove psychologically to the other team that his players were in better shape and not frustrated, no matter how the game was going or which way the calls were falling. In fact, he could only recall once or twice in his entire career when he called the first time-out in a game.

TOURNAMENT PREPARATION. *Did he prepare teams differently for the tournament than for the regular season?* Coach's answer surprised me because it seemed counterintuitive. He would actually cut down on practice time for the NCAA tournament so his players would not get tired, but other than that, he didn't change anything at all. Their preparation had carried them to the tournament; he could trust it to carry them through it, too. And no matter what, he tried not to focus on the opponent. Unconventional perhaps, but clearly effective.

WEIGHT TRAINING. *Did he believe in it? Did he hire a strength coach or have his assistants do it? And when did they lift?* Coach shrugged off this question. He was never an advocate of lifting, and preferred running for conditioning and relying on skills rather than physical strength. He believed he could provide all the conditioning his players needed just through great practices. Basketball conditioning was more important to him than brute strength.

ZONE DEFENSES. *Why did he not use zone defenses, and think man-to-man was better?* Coach didn't appreciate zone defenses except for the zone press, preferring instead to lean on a strong and well-executed man-to-man defense. But if he needed it, he opted for a good, old-fashioned two-three zone. Here, as with everything, he reminded me: "Practice simplicity with constant repetition." He winked. "That, and have better players than everyone else."

THIS WENT ON for days; each night, I would stagger back to my room, and each morning would come back with a fresh list of questions. I also spent time with Coach looking at game video. One day, on our way to his office, we passed his players in a full-court scrimmage, up and down in Pauley Pavilion. It was just a pickup game, the kind most players enjoy in the preseason before practices start. As we walked up the sidelines, Wooden's great All-American Larry Farmer went in for a layup and gracefully eased the ball up over the rim. Wooden came to a screeching halt. Calmly, he turned toward Farmer and told him, "Larry, lay the ball up on the backboard as you were taught." That was all he said, that was all that needed to be said. "Yes, sir," Farmer replied. And we walked on up to his office.

The last day I was there, I went to his house and thanked him and his wife, Nell. I was about to leave when Coach said, "Well, Dale, I'm really glad that you came out, and it's been a delightful time. However, it really wasn't necessary for you to waste your time and money and all those pages of paper, because if you do the following three things, you will be successful in major college basketball. If you don't do them, it will be most difficult." He didn't say it would be impossible—typical of John Wooden—but he said it would be difficult.

I was scrambling for my pen when he said, "Those three

things are fairly simple: Number one, make certain, Dale, you always have better players than anybody you play. Now, with that locked up, make sure you always get the better players to put the team above themselves. And number three—this is very important, Dale Brown," he said, "don't try to be some coaching genius, or give the guys too much information, or too much stuff; always practice simplicity with constant repetition."

I made sure that was not the end of my effort to grow in Coach's mentorship. In fact, I have made that "pilgrimage" to his condo dozens of times, and I stay in touch with him to this day. I love listening to him tell stories, recite poetry. At ninety-nine, he's still animated, sharp, and giving of his time to help others.

From the first time I met him, I understood that by his compassion, by his intellect, his quest to be a teacher, John Wooden would be among my life's most significant mentors. I think Coach could have been just as happy teaching in a small school in Indiana or North Dakota and never coaching. But not until I was ready to take the reins of a program and shoulder the responsibility of being a head coach did I recognize how very much I needed his wisdom. As he has said to me several times, "The teacher can only appear when the student is ready."

Every time I'm in his presence I learn something new. For example, I asked him recently, "Do you think you could have contributed as much if you hadn't won ten National Championships? Would you have been the same sought-after teacher that you are today?" Most people would want to say, "Sure, I'd be the same." Not John Wooden. "Probably not," he said without a moment's hesitation. "Basketball gave me a platform, gave me an opportunity; it was my speaker's stand."

Even as he recognized his fame on a platform from which he might have a positive influence, he also paradoxically shunned the spotlight. I've never seen anyone deflect attention the way he did; it was an incredible lesson in humility. When the media lavished praise on him, he would divert their applause to his players or his assistant coaches or even his past coaches. I remember hearing him on numerous occasions remark, "Oh, that was something I learned from my high school coach." Or, "That was something we did back when I was in college, and I picked it up there." He was never one to let a mentoring opportunity pass him by. Even with the press he would remind his audience that his knowledge had been gained at the feet of someone else.

THE GREATEST LESSON I learned from him, though, was to love what you are doing every day, and to love people. Many times when a waiter was pouring water for us in a restaurant, Coach would say "thank you" while everyone else at the table just kept talking. Everyone feels his love for people—from those he doesn't really know, to his buddies.

Why is the greatest coach not egotistical, selfish, arrogant, and greedy—like so many who reach the pinnacle of what the world often defines as success? In my mind, it is because he firmly believes the definition of the word "successful" from a very early dictionary, in 1806: "fortunate, happy, kind, and prosperous." Coach has often told me that fame, fortune, and power are not success, that the four things mankind craves the most are freedom, happiness, peace, and love, none of which can be obtained without first giving it to someone else.

I've had people ask me, once they learn how closely I was mentored by John Wooden, if his lessons changed the way I mentor others in turn. I know that the "right" answer to that should be, "Of course! He opened my eyes as to how I could be the greatest mentor I can possibly be!" But the truth is, I couldn't hold his gym bag in that realm. I wish I had become a mentor of equal power and magnanimity, but I know I've failed many, many times to live up to his example. Yet that's okay—because mentoring isn't something that happens in one isolated moment. It's the ongoing principles and wisdom by which we conduct our lives and share with others. And yes, that's something I learned from Coach, too.

Perhaps a better way to define Coach is what Einstein said about Gandhi: "Generations to come will scarce believe that such a one as this ever in flesh and blood walked upon the earth." John Wooden is indeed a legend in basketball, but more importantly, he is a legend in serving mankind as a master teacher and mentor. His record stands untouched in college basketball, but the lives he has touched with his mentorship form an enormous family.

SEVERAL YEARS AGO, Coach Wooden and I were asked to speak at a convention in Mexico. My wife said to Coach, "Every time Dale's on the phone with you, he's making notes. I see him writing you letters, he comes out to see you. Has anyone asked you more questions in your lifetime than Dale?"

Coach smiled and said, "Let's just say this: Dale has a lot of interesting questions, and I always wonder where he gets them." Vonnie laughed and asked her follow-up: "Well, Coach, has he picked your mind more than anybody else?" He said, "Well, I suspect he has."

"So with all he's gotten from you," Vonnie pressed, "when you watch his teams play, do you ever sit there and think, 'Didn't he learn anything from me?' " Coach Wooden laughed in a way that I'll never forget. Then he politely didn't answer the question. It had been thirty-seven years since I first sat in his house with my notepad, and I was still learning from him!

·············

CHAPTER 15

Bob Vigars

It amazes me how many letters arrive at my house every day. I haven't coached in nearly four decades, but people still write with a question, and some still ask if they can visit. For years, I have tried to write as many people back as I can, and to see a few folks who can make the trip. Some come more than once, such as Doug Ogle, a basketball coach in one of my old hometowns, South Bend, Indiana. Doug has been out to California seven times to visit with me and discuss coaching. Just the other day I saw a newspaper article about Doug. He was recently facing a difficult point in his career, and he fought back with incredible success. I was so proud reading the story about him, seeing the work he's accomplished, and reading that he believed that our time together helped him in some small way. Some of the greatest letters are from coaches and others I've never had the chance to meet. I never know how I am going to be blessed when that crate of mail is slid onto my back porch, but I am sure that somewhere, there will be a letter that will remind me how important it is to live every day as a mentor. In April 2008, Bob Vigars wrote just such a letter.

—John Wooden

. . . .

I've never met John Wooden, but my students will tell you that I talk about him as if he was my best friend in the world. I quote him all the time—in fact, he is almost like an unseen member of our class, whose wisdom and encouragement are always there, pushing us forward and giving us pause. I can start writing a quotation from John Wooden on the board, and after the first word is up, one of the students will inevitably finish the quote for me. But I've never met the man.

It turns out, that doesn't matter.

I was an active kid who loved to push my teachers' buttons just to see them get riled up; I probably caused a lot of headaches and gray hairs in my school days. Maybe even some early retirements. I guess it was payback, then, when my first job out of university was working with troubled kids, trying to get them in a better position to finish school.

The job was hard and, at times, incredibly depressing. Most of my students had home lives that ranged from awful to unspeakable, and I heard from them again and again that they felt no one listened and no one cared. It made me realize how thankful I was for my own supportive family: two brothers, John and Jim, who are still my best friends, and two loving, supportive parents, Mary-Anne and John. I had been a handful because it was fun. But as I interacted with the children at the center where I worked, I realized that they weren't reacting out of boredom, but from a sense of defeat or desperation.

After reading their student files, learning their histories, or just hearing them talk about their daily struggles, I felt a heavy burden. And yet there was a fulfillment I took from the job. Even if I couldn't make the huge, sweeping changes I had wanted to as a young and idealistic person, I still could have a positive impact just by letting them know that at least one adult cared about them. It didn't take long for me to decide that I wanted to be a full-time teacher to special needs students, helping them in school so they could succeed in life.

As I was completing teacher training and certification, I found myself relying more and more on certain books that were outside the standard assigned curriculum. They weren't written by a famous psychologist or motivational speaker, but their words did more to inspire me and to shape my teaching philosophy than anything else. I am talking, of course, about the writings of John Wooden.

I was first introduced to Coach Wooden's ideas when I was twelve. A grade five teacher named John Lavereau—a young, popular, well-liked guy who I knew coached the basketball team for our school's upper grades—took me aside and let me know in no uncertain terms that he expected better from me than I was giving in my schoolwork and conduct. I had just pulled some big stunt that landed me in a lot of trouble, and Mr. Lavereau warned me, "Bobby, you crossed the line this time. If you continue to go down this road, you will never be on a team I coach."

We sat down and went over Coach Wooden's Pyramid of Success, discussing each aspect and how it might apply to me and my own goals. That really opened my eyes; the amazing coach I watched on TV had a life beyond the court, and his teachings could influence more than just college superstars.

I guess that was one of my first lessons in mentoring, too. Mr. Lavereau took the time to invest in my life by introducing me to a mentor of his own. He had never met John Wooden, either, but he certainly seemed to respect him. That small act, a conversation in the hallway at school and an afternoon of going over the pyramid, made all the difference in the world to me. It didn't make my behavior perfect right away, but it did start shaping the philosophies that would be key in my own teaching career decades down the road.

John Lavereau had introduced me to the reality of "invisible mentors"—people whose lives and writings inspire us, and whose lessons we carry with us in the back of our heads. As my own basketball career began and I started attending camps and clinics around Ontario and the United States, it seemed to me that the one common denominator, no matter the coach, the players, or the techniques being taught, was that John Wooden was quoted, and that everyone agreed his ideas worked. Many of these individuals had enjoyed the opportunity to meet Coach face-to-face, but many more had not. And yet they all seemed to have learned from him.

Most of us rely on invisible mentors already, even if we're not aware of it. Most kids have a hero they admire and try to emulate. Even if it's just through sports skills or a way of dressing, they are still adopting a part of a persona they admire, making it part of their own identity.

As we grow older, we often find ourselves moved by quotations we've heard or inspired by stories we've read about great individuals and common people accomplishing great things. What I think is so important is that we recognize those bits of wisdom as real learning opportunities and allow ourselves to be mentored by them.

Coach Wooden has become an invisible mentor to my students both on the court and in the classroom because the lessons he has taught through word and action have shaped my own life and how I teach. So many of the lessons I apply aren't my own; they're taken straight from one of Coach's books or from his Pyramid of Success. And because most of my kids are eager for a mentor to show them how to get ready for life, they soak up that wisdom. They know that his lessons aren't always easy, but they are valuable.

For example, the St. Joseph's Junior Boys Basketball team I coach, which consists of boys ages thirteen to fifteen, recently made it to the regional playoffs. As a team, we agreed that no one was going to miss a single practice as we went into tournament play; but our star player shrugged off practice one night to take his girlfriend out. I hated the thought of playing without him, but Coach Wooden always insists that the bench is a coach's best friend, and I took that to heart; that young man did not play the next game. He suited up and sat on the sidelines, but I didn't allow him to take the court. He and his parents were very upset about that decision, but I reminded him of Coach Wooden's simple truth, "Nobody is bigger than the team."

We won that game, and then won several more in the following days with all of our team playing. In fact, we made it to the final round, losing only in the championship game. Facing the same team we had previously lost to by twenty-seven points, with only one practice, this time we lost by only four points. I was ecstatic; that was the greatest loss of my life! As I told the players in the locker room, they had played an amazing game, their best ever. And that loss was one they could all be incredibly proud of because it perfectly embodied Coach Wooden's definition of success.

And wouldn't you know it, the same player I had benched a few days before came up to me, gave me a huge hug, and said, "If it wasn't for you, Vigs"—that's my nickname—"I never would have learned the hardest lesson of my life. I will never miss another practice."

———————

BUT THE LESSONS I've learned from John Wooden aren't limited to my basketball team. In my classroom, where I work with adolescent students—mostly between ages nine and fifteen—who are facing emotional, behavioral, and learning challenges, I find that the mentoring lessons from Coach are every bit as applicable.

On the first day of class, I look out at the faces in front of me and tell them, "Right now, you probably feel like ants. You've been stepped on by people in your life who didn't think you were good enough or important enough. But guess what?" Then I jump onto a desk and say: "We aren't going to be ants anymore. We are going to be giraffes, or rhinos, or whatever animals you want to be as long as it is too big to get stepped on." They laugh at me, because I probably look and sound a little ridiculous, but that laughter starts a bond between us, and the use of the word "we" lets them know that I'm in this with them. We're a team, and every single piece of the engine has a part in making the car (or the class) move forward.

I often remind my students of the importance of teamwork, of feeling connected with their peers and working together to reach their shared goal. I encourage them to "be the best you can be every day." Some days will be more difficult than others, but by focusing on trying to get something out of every day, even if it is just something small, that's an important step in becoming the best possible version of themselves.

With many of my students struggling to catch up to their peers in emotional maturity, sometimes the best they can be each day isn't someone who finishes a book or masters a new concept in mathematics, but someone who can be open to learning. Other students are dealing with much larger personal battles than any child their age should have to face, and some days their minds can't engage with the lesson. I remind them that not all days can be great ones but that they should still strive to be the best person their emotions and circumstances will allow them to be that day and that we'll try to make the next day even better.

Often, my students come to my class discouraged because they have been told they aren't smart enough to learn in a regular classroom. After years of falling behind through learning disabilities or from dealing with emotional issues, they have been put on a specialized track geared to address each student's individual issues. I always remind them that it's not that we can't learn, it's that we learn differently. And here I turn to the one quote from Coach Wooden that I probably rely on more than anything else: "Nothing will work unless you do."

It is essential to my teaching that my students have a sense of ownership and responsibility in their own education. I know they can learn; all of them can. But because they have been crushed by circumstances, most of them have fallen into the trap of thinking that something is wrong with them, or broken in their mind. I insist that they not get caught in the trap of "can't." Of course they will face concepts—maybe even entire disciplines—that will be difficult, but that doesn't mean they are unable to learn; it just means they can't accept the fact that the ability does exist inside them.

To help them move from thinking "I can't" to realizing that it's more just a case of "I won't," I write that quote from Coach Wooden on the board and ask them what it means to them. Once they reason their way through it, each student starts to realize that his or her attitude is causing their individual learning challenges. If they are willing to accept that they can learn, then we've taken the first step to actually learning.

It is such a simple phrase, yet so powerful in its succinctness. As each student sounds it out, that's one victory; they were able to read it. When they offer their analysis of it, that's a second victory; they were able to comprehend its meaning and apply it to their own situation. And as they start to embrace what it's saying by changing their mind-set, that's a third victory; they are doing the work that success requires. I return to that quote again and again in my instruction. Sometimes my students will get wrapped around a particularly challenging lesson and want me to just fill in the answer rather than walking them through the steps of solving it. "I can't pick up your pencil," I tell them. "The day I do that, they'd better fire me instantly because you're not learning anything. Doing the work makes the difference between learning and not learning."

Often they struggle with emotional outbursts from frustration or an unwillingness to accept authority. I stress discipline in my classroom, but explain to my students that I am not punishing them. Punishment is something that hurts. Instead, I am making them face the consequences of their choices through extra instruction at lunch, recess, or after school. I remind them of Coach's statement, "Discipline yourself and others won't have to." This helps each student be mindful of his or her responsibility to exercise self-control. That is a real struggle for many of my students, but they come to understand the message of that statement and they see the truth behind it.

Coach Wooden also talks a lot about the importance of writing down goals so they can serve as visual reminders of what you're working toward. I do that with my goals for each basketball season, and I help my students do that, too, with a progress chart called "Choose Respect and Responsibility." Starting at the beginning of each marking period, they get different colored Xs for different behavioral infractions, and they all know that the goal is to have a clear chart. That goal keeps them accountable because they see the chart hanging on the wall, making them mindful of what they are aiming for. It's a very simple system, but it is an effective one. Coach's emphasis on keeping goals in mind has helped me explain to my classes how to strive for continual improvement.

I know it makes a difference because my students contact me within a few weeks of leaving my class, or years later, and let me know how they're doing. In fact, I am in touch with almost all of my former students and players, and they are all grateful for those lessons in how to change their attitudes—from believing they can't do something to realizing that with a little effort, they truly can.

Coach Wooden's mentoring in my life reaches beyond the classroom and into my home. One of my boys' favorite bedtime stories is Coach Wooden's children's book *Inch and Miles*, which has allowed my wife, Shanna, and me to share with them the same lessons that helped shape my own growing up. In fact, Joshua is now old enough that he can read along with me, and we take turns reading as if we were each of the characters. Sometimes he's Inch and sometimes he's Miles, and it thrills me to see him get excited about the lessons he's learning. I can't wait until Kristopher is old enough to read along, too. I can see Coach Wooden's mentoring influence on their lives, even at such an early age, as they absorb the simple truths in the book and start to make them their own rules for living.

My letter to Coach Wooden was just one of hundreds that come into his house each month, and from what I understand, most of those letters read much like mine. We've all been mentored by the life of Coach Wooden, and we all have taken to heart the wisdom he has shared with us in the form of books, quotes, and even just the quiet testimony of his humble and godly spirit. He may have retired years ago, but his words and his example have continued to change lives. John Wooden doesn't just mentor people; he also shows us how to become mentors ourselves. That's one of the greatest gifts one human being can give to another.

CHAPTER 16
. . . .
Cori Nicholson

Just six months after Nellie passed away in 1985, the empty-feeling home we had lived in together was filled again with love and energy. In September of that year, my granddaughter Caryn gave birth to my first great-grandchild, Cori. Shortly after Cori's birth, Caryn and her husband separated, and I invited Caryn and Cori to live with me for a few weeks until they got situated. At seventy-five years old, I learned again how to change diapers.

When Cori was eleven, in 1996, she got her ears pierced. She knew I didn't think that was a good idea and she tried to hide her ears from me . . . but I knew. I realized that the decision was already made, so the best thing I could do was let her know I loved her. So we got in the car and went to the mall, where I offered to let her pick out some earrings, little diamond solitaires. On the way home, she said, "PaPa, I hope you live for five more years." Her statement made me chuckle, but it also made me curious. "Why is that?" I asked. "Because I'll be sixteen then, and you're the one I want to take me to get my driver's license."

She's not a big fan of that story, but I love that she wanted me to be part of her big moments.

She's more like my wife than any of my other great-grandchildren are. I'm close to her in a different way. I don't love her any more or any less than the others, but her arrival was so important to me and came at such a special time. I needed love in the house right then, and there she was.

—John Wooden

. . . .

John Wooden is my great-grandfather, but like his other twelve great-grandchildren, I just call him PaPa. He tells that story about me when I was eleven years old all the time, and frankly I'm a little bit embarrassed by it. It was such a dumb thing to say. I don't ever again want to pick a date that he has to live to because I really want him to live forever. That's selfish, I know. I've always known that when we lose him, he'll get the chance to spend eternity with his wife.

As a little girl, I knew that PaPa was special to us, but I never understood that he was famous. My mom, he, and I would go out to dinner, and every time, without fail, someone we didn't know would come to the table and ask for an autograph. (Weirdly, no one made autograph requests when I went to dinner with my other grandparents.) My PaPa would never say no. He often drove me to preschool or picked me up to go shopping, and everywhere we went, people would want to come up and talk to him. I always wondered why.

I was born ten years after my PaPa retired from coaching. I never got to see him do what made him famous to other people. To me, he was famous for his Waldorf salad at Christmas. We used to get really excited when he would let us help make that salad. Everybody thinks he's an amazing coach, but they should also know he makes an amazing Waldorf salad!

As I grew older, I heard the stories about all he'd done, and it started to make sense. He wasn't just my PaPa, he also was someone truly special. It was hard for me to see that for the longest time. I mean, he changed my diapers.

I WAS A good student as a kid. If you go into my PaPa's condo even today you'll see my preschool report card on his wall. I could count to twenty-nine! But in high school I went through a rebellious I'm-not-going-to-do-schoolwork stage. As he would say, I was preparing to fail. Those couple of years kept me from getting into UCLA. They rejected me because my grades weren't good enough.

Coming out of high school I thought I wanted to be a pediatrician. But after a few classes at UC Riverside, I realized that wasn't for me. When I was trying to decide what to do with my life, I remembered how PaPa would often say that teaching was the ultimate profession, the ultimate gift to other people. I went to him and asked, "PaPa, would you be upset if I decided to change my major? I've decided I want to be a teacher." And he said, "Upset, honey? Listen, I think that's exactly what you're cut out to be."

Several people in our family have been teachers. All three of PaPa's brothers were. To him, it really is the greatest profession. It turned out to be a blessing in disguise that I had landed at UC Riverside, because it has a fabulous education program. I finished my bachelor's degree in liberal studies in 2007 and my masters in education in 2008. I am proud to say I am now a kindergarten teacher in Riverside County, California.

Lots of people talk about the fact that my PaPa referred to himself as a teacher and not a coach. That was because he took time to teach everyone, not just his players. As far back as I can remember, he would encourage us to bring friends over to join in family events. And when we did, he always would want to teach them or tell them something. He always would talk to my friends one-on-one. A lot of adults address children as non-thinkers, as something less than a full person. Not PaPa. He always talked directly to my friends, and that respect allowed them to learn from him.

So many people have learned from the way he coached. I learned by watching how he lived his life, from the example he set every day. From him I learned that mentoring is more about living than it is about talking.

My PaPa is a lifelong learner; he's always looking for new things to discover and new things to teach. When I was young, I thought he knew everything, but he always made sure we understood that wasn't the case.

Through him, I realized that learning more each day is important, and that teaching is best done when the teacher finds a way to make learning interesting. He always tried to make everything sound fascinating, even when he knew we were not particularly interested. I apply that lesson every day as I work to make things engaging for my students. It's rewarding to see them get excited about things they wouldn't normally be excited about. If I can make learning valuable and make it apply to their life, they will take ownership of it. When I see that in their eyes, I know I have just handed them a lesson from PaPa.

Another of the lessons I learned from my PaPa is to look for ways to make things relatable to my students—how to make the things I teach relevant to their life by accessing their prior knowledge. For instance, we were talking about numbers recently, and I have a chart on my wall counting from one to one hundred. We were counting to see when we would get to the one-hundredth day of school. I could tell that the students didn't have good number concepts at that age, so I said, "Let's see . . . how old are you guys? How old am I? And do you want to see how old my grandpa is?" I went all the way up to ninety-eight, and they were shocked. I think they connected with it because it wasn't just a number, because it was something I was talking about personally. To this day, they still ask, "Miss Nicholson, how old is your grandpa? Can we point to it?"

WHILE A LOVE of learning is a great gift from PaPa, I can see other ways he has mentored me in my daily life. In several of these areas, he is so much better than I am that it is challenging to figure out how to meet the expectations he has set. Take the art of being gracious: In my twenty-three years of life, I can honestly say I have never seen my PaPa be cross with anyone; he may be a smart aleck, but I've never seen him be mean. Think of all the records he has to his name, all the trophies in his house, all the certificates on the wall . . . none of those is as an impressive a record as the one he has set for his treatment of others.

Another amazing thing about PaPa is that he never judges anyone. No matter who you are, you're worth his time and effort. I think that's a really amazing standard to live up to, and it's a good example in education as well. A lot of my students are disadvantaged; some of them live in a single rented room with their parents. But in my classroom, I have to make sure they're all equal.

PaPa also is unbelievably giving of his time. I recently did a fund-raiser with the Leukemia and Lymphoma Society. My best friend's little girl has leukemia and had just finished her chemo. There were only seven people fund-raising, and all of us asked

everyone we knew for money. PaPa was first to make a dona-
tion. Then, at the end of the event, there was a live auction, and
PaPa offered to auction off a lunch or dinner with him. A bid-
ding war developed between two people. He decided he would
do two dinners, and we sold them both. That whole event
raised a lot of money, but we wouldn't have done nearly as
well without his willingness to make his time available for our
cause.

I truly believe that if he had been an amazing coach, but also
a jerk, nobody would even keep him in mind now. It's because
he was such an amazing teacher—and coach, and player, and
an amazing man—that everybody still wants to enjoy him today.

PaPa is well known for the sayings he has used over the years.
People have turned them into calendars, used them in books,
quoted them in speeches. Everyone seems to have a favorite.
I do, too: *Make each day your masterpiece.* Work to make the
most of today, then do the same tomorrow and, over time,
things will come together. And if you were to make each day a
masterpiece, you would make a lifetime of amazing memories.
That's something he's lived up to. And it's something I want to
live up to, too.

The saying means so much to me that earlier this year, I decided to make it part of me permanently; I got it tattooed on the
inside of my left wrist! I keep it covered at school with my
watch, but I always know it's there.

Not long after I got the tattoo, I told my mom and I thought
she was going to be really angry. What happened was even worse.
She said, "I'm telling PaPa." As you might imagine, my PaPa is not
into tattoos. The next time I saw him, my mom grabbed me and
made me show him. He just shook his head—the same look I got

when he found out I had had my ears pierced at eleven. I could see in his eyes that he disapproved, but he didn't say it.

I figured the best way to get him to forget my little tattoo was to suggest something worse. I joked that my brother was going to get a tattoo of the Pyramid of Success on his back!

I NEVER HAD the chance to see my PaPa and his wife, Nellie, hold hands. She went to heaven the same year I was born. But I have spent hours at PaPa's knee listening to him talk about her. She was his true love, and he was her best friend.

The year this book is written, 2009, is the year I get married. And of all the lessons I hope I can take from PaPa—of all the places where I hope his mentoring sticks—this is the one that's most important to me. I absolutely dream about building the kind of never-ending love that they maintained. I've never heard of any other two people being so intertwined that they practically become one person. When he talks about her, eighty-plus years after they first fell in love, his eyes still get misty. It's something special to see. Many people know that he writes her a love letter on the twenty-first day of every month (that was the date she passed away) and has every month since 1985. As I grew up in his home, I stared at that growing stack of letters, wondering what kind of love it takes to maintain that commitment and looking forward to the day when I could find someone I'd want to write to that way.

He was seventy-five—still pretty young—when she passed away, and women were after him. But there was just no way. He was completely devoted to her. My fiancé, Brett, and I joke that because his grandma is six years younger than PaPa, we think they should date. . . . But it would never happen. We both know there's no one else for him.

In 2009, when Gatorade asked my PaPa to be part of its television commercials rebranding the drink as "G," the director Spike Lee asked each of the stars in the commercials to name their "G moment," their biggest accomplishment. Most of them claimed a big championship; for example, Serena Williams said hers was winning Wimbledon.

PaPa didn't handle the question like the rest of them. He said, "It's when my late wife said 'I do.' " Everyone on the set, including Spike Lee, stopped what they were doing because they could feel his love.

I only got to know half of the John and Nellie Wooden team, but the two of them have set an example of love that is my goal. As I become the first Wooden great-grandchild to enter marriage, I have promised PaPa and my new husband, Brett, that those lessons of love are ones I'm holding closest to my heart.

CHAPTER 17
. . . .

Closing Thoughts

As I finish this book, I am nearly ninety-eight and a half years old. I believe that in the first five years of your life and the last five of your first hundred, you should be able to record your age in fractions.

Sometimes I'm asked whether at this age I can still have a mentor. The answer is simple: Of course I can! The day I stop learning from others is the day I'll head to see my Nellie in heaven. As I hope most will agree after reading this book, the greatest learning occurs when you've selected proper mentors. The seven people mentioned in the first half of this book, through my constant thoughts of them, surely offer a good start.

But I am also mentored today by my son Jim, and granddaughter Caryn Bernstein. When I fell one night and became injured in 2008, the two of them adjusted their lives and their schedules to split each week and move into my home with me. While both had been regular parts of my daily life before that, the sudden twenty-four-hour companionship allowed for far more conversation, laughter, and learning than previously.

Jim is so much like my dad. I say with all sincerity that I wish

I were as good a person as my son. I have learned so much about patience from him during this situation. Despite what a drain I must be now on him and his family, he is always positive. He never has a negative thing to say about anybody, never a profane word. Just being around him keeps my spirits high. For him to maintain that attitude all day every day makes him a role model to me.

Caryn is one of my seven grandchildren, and as a group they're the greatest set of grandchildren a man can ask for. Because of our time together, I've learned so much from her, too. Her patience with me is a constant source of amazement and of teaching. She's tough but patient. That's a great combination. She has fun with me and reminds me to laugh, which is so important. Her mother, my daughter Nan, is much like Nellie. She has given much of her adult life to looking after me, to making sure I'm protected, which may sound like an odd thing. But she always is making sure I am active and involved in positive projects. Nell protected me, too.

In fact, following my fall in February of 2008, when I broke my wrist and collarbone, a number of my family and friends came together to divide up their time in order to keep someone at my house just in case I needed them. Up until that point, I had always fought for my independence, insisting that I didn't need around-the-clock care. They haven't made it feel like monitoring, though; it's been more like just having a series of wonderful companions to keep me company throughout the day. My children and grandchildren have been such a blessing in that regard.

One of the most dedicated of my friends has been Tony Spino, a longtime trainer at UCLA. He has volunteered to work with me, often even spending the night in order to make sure that the next morning, my muscles are stretched and massaged. Weak as they may be, Tony always manages to get my limbs and joints moving so that I can take care of whatever is on my agenda that day. Our mutual love of baseball gives us a lot to talk about, but his unwavering patience with me is a tremendous lesson from which I continue to learn and grow every day.

My father helped me define success as peace of mind. To have peace of mind, you've got to try to live the kind of life you think will open the gates for you in heaven. Yet you know there will be times along the way when you don't have the patience you should have. I tried to teach my players this: When the game is over, it's over, and it won't be replayed. But regardless of the score, if you know you made the best effort you could, we won. If each one of you feels that, we may be outscored, but I can't ask any more than for you to make the effort to do the best you can. That doesn't mean just the time on the floor, but also all the preparation.

IF YOU TRY to make the effort, you will have peace with yourself. My peace assures that I'm not afraid of death. I'm not going to intentionally hurry it up, but I'm not afraid of it. I think at least part of my longevity is because I have peace within myself.

I would say that I've had that peace for most of my life, with a few short stretches when it was missing. The most pronounced was when I lost Nellie. After she passed, I had regrets, which is something we had promised each other we wouldn't have. But there were things I wished I had done for Nellie, and there were things I wished I hadn't done. Nellie loved to dance, but I never learned, and I wished I had. And I wished I hadn't enlisted in the service without talking to her first. I didn't involve her enough in that decision, and it hurt her.

It isn't that I love Nellie; I'm in love with Nellie. Even today, I am in love with her.

———

As I WROTE in the first chapter, I wanted this book to recognize and honor Nellie and the other mentors who were most significant in my life. And as I wrote in chapter nine, I also wanted this book to recognize seven people who have used that great word to describe me.

But I would be remiss if I didn't also recognize you, the reader of this book. Maybe you picked it up because you care about basketball, or because you saw some names that interested you, or maybe you were reminded of a role model in your own life. Whatever the case, you have what it takes to learn at the feet of someone else, and to offer up your own life lessons to the next generation. You have the potential—no, you have the responsibility—to be a mentor and to be mentored.

And so I write this book for you, too. Thank you for making this commitment.

Acknowledgments

One of the most amazing things about Coach John Wooden is that he may be listed as author on more books while in his nineties than just about anyone who has ever been published. Such is the enduring value of his life and the lessons he teaches. That fact gives anyone working with him a treasure trove of details, but does present its own challenge: With so much written by and about Coach, how do you unearth stories and angles that haven't yet been spelled out for his reading public? How do you keep this from being another book built on all those same stories, as some authors have done? When Pat Williams, the longtime GM of the Orlando Magic and the author of a critically acclaimed biography of Coach Wooden, read this manuscript, his words suggested we had overcome this challenge. "I interviewed seven hundred people for my book," Williams said, referring to *How to Be Like Coach Wooden.* "And you had stories there I hadn't heard. Congratulations!"

For that to happen, I had to lean on an amazing team of researchers and great writers who work with me, led by the always precise Tiffany Yecke-Brooks. As she pored over all that's been written by Coach, Tiffany chronicled the hundreds of stories told previously so that we could take the more than one hundred hours of taped interviews with Coach used for this book and make sure that we picked the best and "freshest" stories to share here. Jim Henry, a star journalist in his own right, and Jenny Fernandez also helped craft this project.

Former LSU coach Dale Brown, who is featured here as one of those whose life has been shaped by Coach, was key to the early development of this project. His love for Coach Wooden and his passion for mentoring were key to making this happen. Each of the seven mentees who participated here gave of their time freely out of respect for Coach, and this book would have been incomplete without their dedication and openness.

Three others who were integral to this book's success were agent Doug Grad, who believed in the project from day one, and Bloomsbury's Nick Trautwein and George Gibson. Nick slaved over most of the manuscript before taking another job, then left it in George's able hands. This book is immeasurably better for their work.

Finally, though, I have to thank Coach Wooden's daughter, Nan and son, Jim. Whenever a challenge arose, these two made sure that telling this story about their father's legacy as mentor would happen. No one could stop this project with Nan and Jim as its engine!

Index

A Note on the Authors

JOHN WOODEN is the most successful basketball coach in NCAA history, having led the UCLA Bruins to 665 victories and ten championships in the years leading up to 1975. Since his retirement, he has become a mentor to dozens of athletes, journalists, and writers, and the author of nine books.

DON YAEGER is the author or coauthor of sixteen books, including *Never Die Easy*, with Walter Payton, and *Running for My Life*, with Warrick Dunn.